Ines Sche

D0373595

Aquarium Plants Manual

Expert advice on selection, planting, care, and propagation

Consulting Editor: Dennis W. Stevenson. Director, Harding Laboratory, The New York Botanical Garden

Color Photographs: Burkard Kahl and A. van den Nieuwenhuizen

Drawings: Marlene Gemke

BARRON'S

Contents

*Preceding pages:
A plant aquarium
with a splendid
array of cardinal
flowers (fore-
ground), along
with delicate fish
species.*

*Anubias barteri a
decorative plant of
which there are
several different
varieties.*

Preface

What makes an aquarium a true focus of attention in your home? Is it the brightly colored fish? They aren't the sole attraction! Richly abundant water plants also catch the observer's eye. Barron's aquarium expert Ines Scheurmann explains in this book what you need to know about plants for your aquarium. Proper maintenance of the water—the vital element—is the *sine qua non* for the growth of the plants. The accessories used in the aquarium—the lights, heaters, and filters—have to be exactly right. Choosing the water plants and expertly placing them in the bottom material also play an important role in setting up an aquarium. On "How-To" pages that include vivid drawings, you will be given important tips on planting, along with suggested plant layouts that will stimulate your imagination. In addition, you will learn what guidelines to follow in tending and propagating the plants and how to control diseases and pests. A detailed glossary will give you quick access to all the important terms and concepts having to do with the underwater world of the plants. Finally, in the section on plant profiles you can acquire specific information about the most beautiful aquarium plants, which are pictured there in full-color photographs.

The author and the editors of Barron's series of nature books wish you a great deal of pleasure with your aquarium plants.

Please see the **Important Notes** *on page 93.*

3

What You Need to Know About Aquarium Plants

Why Plants Are Important in an Aquarium

Aquarium plants produce oxygen, absorb the carbon dioxide produced by the fish, and help in the breakdown of waste materials. By so doing, the plants make a substantial contribution to the creation of a stable environment in the aquarium.

The water hyacinth (Eichhornia crassipes) *has sweet-smelling blue flowers.*

How Plants Produce Oxygen

With the help of the green pigment in their leaves—chlorophyll—plants are able to use sunlight as a source of energy. In their green parts, plants make from water and carbon dioxide the carbohydrates of which they themselves are composed. In this process, known as photosynthesis, oxygen is released—in a manner of speaking, as a by-product of this assimilation. Because most of the oxygen we breathe is produced by green (chlorophyll-containing) plants—namely, algae, mosses, ferns, flowering plants, deciduous trees, and conifers—neither humans nor other animals can live without plants.

Only after the first single-celled algae with chlorophyll developed, some two and one-half to three billion years ago, could the development of animal life forms also begin. Before that time there existed only microorganisms and bacteria, which made do with the small amount of oxygen present in the primordial atmosphere or were able to live without oxygen altogether.

How Plants Breathe

Plants not only assimilate, and thereby generate oxygen, they also respire. Just as animals do, plants take in oxygen and give off carbon dioxide. Photosynthesis occurs only in the daytime or when the plants are adequately lit. That is, they are able to assimilate and to produce oxygen only if they have sufficient light. Respiration, however, is a continuous process, occurring day and night.

What Else Plants Can Do

• In an aquarium plants clean the water by absorbing the waste materials that are introduced when the fish eliminate waste products or when fish food is added to the water.

• Many plants contain bactericidal substances with which they can make even bacteria-contaminated water habitable for fish.

• Healthy plants, by giving off small amounts of oxygen in the area surrounding their roots, keep the bottom material from decaying.

• Bacteria and smaller algae settle on the plants, and they too can clean the water.

The lotus lily (Nymphaea lotus) *belongs to the water-lily family.*

Most aquarium plants belong to the most highly developed group of plants, the one that contains the most species: the flowering plants.

These plants
- have roots, stems, leaves, and flowers,
- reproduce by seeds,
- possess complicated vascular and supporting systems composed of highly differentiated types of cells.

Tip: Mosses, ferns, and algae are simpler in structure.

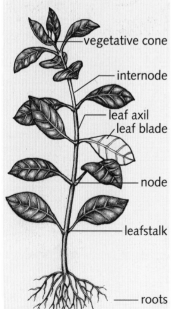

1. *Plant structure; The example shown here is a stem plant.*

vegetative cone

internode

leaf axil
leaf blade

node

leafstalk

roots

Plant Structure
Drawing 1

The above-ground, or aerial, stem of flowering plants consists of the stem axis, the leaves, and the flowers.

Stem axis is the term botanists use for the main axis of every plant, whether it is the delicate stem of a *Limnophila* species or the trunk of a giant sequoia (*Sequoiadendron giganteum*). The tip of the stem, the growth zone of the plant, is called the vegetative point or shoot apex. Stem axes may be elongated or greatly shortened.
- Stem plants have an elongated stem axis, on which the leaves occur at intervals (nodes) with enough distance between them to permit the stem internodes to be visible.
- Rosette plants have a shortened stem internode—that is, the leaves are so close together that they form a basal leaf rosette.

Leaves arise from the stem axis. They consist of the blade (the part we call the leaf) and the leafstalk, or petiole. In plants with elongated stem axes, the points at which the leaves arise are often thickened. These points are called nodes (in Latin, *nodi*). The leafless parts of the stem between the nodes are known as the internodes.

The leaves may be arranged on the stem in various ways (see Drawing 2).

2. *Leaf arrangement: 1. basal leaf rosette; 2. decussate leaves in a stem plant; 3. whorled leaves in a stem plant.*

The side, or lateral, branches of the stem axis develop from buds in the leaf axils.

On the upper side of the leaf blades, the green leafstalks, and the green stems is found the assimilating tissue that contains chlorophyll. It is here that photosynthesis takes place. On the underside of the leaves of land plants and on the emergent leaves of marsh plants are located the stomata, which the plant can cause to expand or contract. Gaseous interchange is accomplished through these openings; that is carbon dioxide (CO_2) is taken in and oxygen (O_2) and water vapor are discharged. Typical underwater leaves have no stomata; gases are interchanged over the entire leaf surface.

The root anchors the plant underground and absorbs nutrients from the soil.

Storage organs are present in various aquarium plants. The sugars produced during photosynthesis are usually converted to starch right in the leaves. Part of this starch is stored in the leaves, part in the stem axis or in separate storage organs. Various forms of storage organs occur in aquatic plants:

• Thickened underground portions of the stem axis, called rhizomes (for example, in *Echinodorus* species).

• Tubers arising from the stem axis (for example, in *Aponogeton* species).

• Bulbs (for example, in *Crinum* species).

Flowers are responsible for reproduction and for propagation by seed.

The reproductive organs— that is, the stamens (male) and the carpels (female)—are located on the thickened tip of the stem axis (floral axis) and are surrounded by asexual, usually colored involucral leaves or petals.

Arrangement of Leaves
Drawing 2
In stem plants the leaves are arranged in various ways: alternate, decussate, or whorled.

In rosette plants the leaves form a basal leaf rosette.

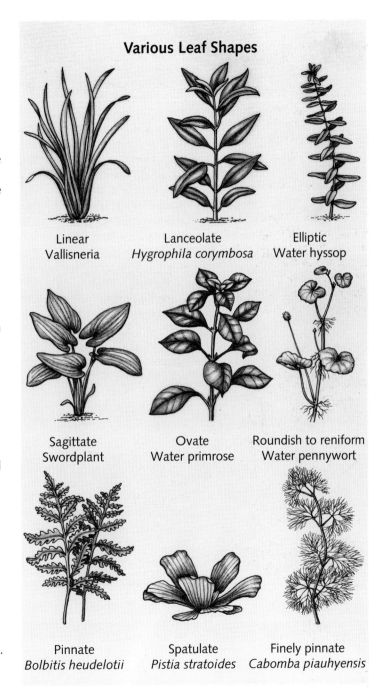

Various Leaf Shapes

Linear
Vallisneria

Lanceolate
Hygrophila corymbosa

Elliptic
Water hyssop

Sagittate
Swordplant

Ovate
Water primrose

Roundish to reniform
Water pennywort

Pinnate
Bolbitis heudelotii

Spatulate
Pistia stratoides

Finely pinnate
Cabomba piauhyensis

Adaptation to Life in Water

Aquatic plants have a very highly developed system of air cavities or canals. It runs through the entire plant, from the leaves to the outermost root tips, and enables the plant to maintain buoyancy in the water. Because the water supports the plants, their stems and leaves have far less supporting tissue or fibers than those of land plants.

In water plants, as in land plants, the upper surfaces of the leaves, which are turned toward the light, are brighter green in color than the undersides of the leaves, because the upper surface layer cells contain the bulk of the chlorophyll.

The protective layer, or cuticle, that covers the leaves and stems keeps land plants from drying up. In water plants, however, this layer is so thin and delicate that these plants can absorb gases and nutrients from the water directly through the surface of the leaves and stems.

Adaptation to the Natural Habitat

Not all plants that can be grown in aquariums are aquatic plants in the true sense. Many grow in marshy or swampy areas or in bodies of water with seasonal fluctuations in the water level. For several months every year they stand out of the water or at least extend above the surface of the water. Therefore we distinguish between aquatic and marsh plants, or between submersed and emergent plants.

Submersed applies to plants or plant parts that are always under water.

Emergent refers to plants or plant parts that rise above the water surface.

Aquatic Plants

Aquatic plants are permanently submersed, and their leaves are thin and delicate. In many species the leaves are pinnate or highly laciniate, so that a large total surface area is created. Typical examples of aquatic plants are *Egeria* and *Elodea* species (waterweed) and *Ceratophyllum* species (hornwort). Aquatic plants are able to absorb gases and nutrients directly from the water.

The leaves of Crinum natans.

The roots in many species are mere clasping organs or are altogether vestigial. Hornwort, for example, has no roots at all; this plant anchors itself in the groud by means of modified leaves.

The flowers of aquatic plants, however, grow emergent, as they generally are pollinated by winged insects or airborne pollen.

Marsh Plants

Only during the wet season do these plants live more or less immersed in water (submersed). As the water level drops they stand entirely or partially emergent; that is, they rise out of the water. During this time they put forth hard, firm emergent leaves, and they take in water and nutrients only through their roots.

Their emergent stems and leaves are similar in structure to those of land plants, but in order to thrive they need higher atmospheric humidity than the latter.

Their submersed leaves are more delicate than those of the emersed plants, but much coarser than those of the typical aquatics. In most species the leaves are entire-margined, only rarely lobate or crenate. Typical examples are *Echinodorus* species (Amazon swordplants) and *Cryptocoryne* species. Marsh plants absorb the principal share of their nutrients through their roots from the bottom of the body of water, even when they are grown submersed in an aquarium. For this reason, they grow best there if the bottom material has been fertilized beforehand.

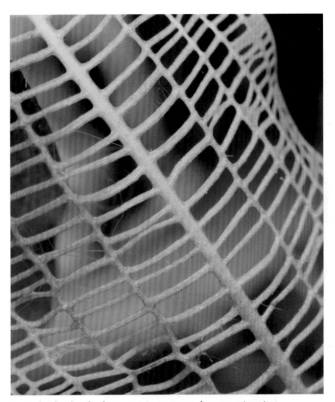

Detail of a leaf of Aponogeton madagascariensis.

Their flowers grow emersed. Many species (*Cryptocoryne*, for example) bear flowers and fruits only if the seasonal fluctuations in the water level are simulated in the aquarium.

Tip: On pages 62 to 89 you will find detailed descriptions of popular aquarium plants and individual instructions for their care. All the plants described are shown in full-color photos.

The marvelously beautiful Aponogeton madagascariensis *comes from Madagascar. In its native habitat this plant has become quite rare. Because it is very difficult to grow, only truly experienced aquarists should try to cultivate it in their tanks.*

Proper Maintenance of the Water–the Vital Element

The quality of the water determines whether your aquarium plants thrive and multiply abundantly or become stunted and die. When choosing plants, also keep in mind that members of a species have identical or similar requirements with regard to water conditions.

In addition to the requirements for light and warmth, the plants' vital element—water—has to be attuned to their needs.

Oxygen (O_2)

Oxygen (O_2) is the greatest vital necessity for all organisms. Plants and animals must have it in order to breathe. Filter bacteria, which break down waste materials such as left-over fish food and fish excreta and convert them into substances that are not toxic for fish, can do their job only if enough O_2 is available.

The oxygen dissolved in the water comes partly from the air; part also is produced by the plants during photosynthesis. In general, water and air are in a state of gas equilibrium with one another; that is, oxygen from the air diffuses into the water if the water contains too little O_2. If too much O_2 is dissolved in the water, the oxygen escapes into the air. Under such equilibrium, about 9 milligrams of O_2 are dissolved in 1 quart (1 L) of water.

Optimum oxygen content, the level at which fish and plants are best able to thrive, is 5 to 7 milligrams of O_2 per quart (L) of water (in the daytime, when photosynthesis is possible). Most aquariums with especially luxuriant vegetation have O_2 values in this range.

Testing the O_2 content: Test kits with which you can determine the O_2 content of the water are available in pet stores. Because a great deal of O_2 is produced in planted aquariums during the daytime in the course of photosynthesis, the O_2 content usually is lower in the morning than in the evening. If you measure the O_2 content in the mornings and afternoons, you will have a criterion for the productivity of your plants.

Care: Try to reach the optimum O_2 content of 5 to 7 milligrams per quart (L) of water. This effort is most apt to succeed in tanks with many plants, few fish, and clean water.

Oxygen Deficiency

This occasionally occurs in poorly maintained aquariums, including:

• too large a fish population and only a few plants,

• dirty and clogged filters, muddy bottom material, and large accumulations of leftover food,

• poor lighting, which reduces photosynthesis capability,

• starved plants, suffering from mineral deficiencies.

In such cases oxygen does pass from the air into the water, but the deficit cannot be corrected quickly enough. If the O_2 content is less than 2 milligrams per quart (L) of water, the fish will be at the surface of the water gasping for air, and the filter bacteria will do their job either too slowly or not at all (see page 48).

Care: If there is a persistent deficiency of O_2, you will have to make radical improvements in the entire aquarium environment.

Oxygen Surplus

In very well-maintained aquariums an excess of oxygen may develop, for example:
• in densely planted tanks with only a few fish,
• in tanks with clean water and properly maintained filters,
• in tanks in which the plants have an optimum supply of light, warmth, and nutrients.

In such cases photosynthesis often is carried out so quickly that the O_2 content rises to more than 9 milligrams per quart (L) of water. Then the excess oxygen gradually escapes into the air. Aquarium water with such a high concentration of oxygen, however, no longer has sufficient nourishment for the plants.

Care: If the oxygen surplus persists, reduce the amount of light: Turn off one fluorescent light or buy tubes with lower output.

Carbon Dioxide (CO_2)

The most vital plant nutrient, carbon dioxide (CO_2), must be present in sufficient quantity in your aquarium if the plants are to thrive.

Monitoring the CO_2 content: There are various possibilities:
• Drop indicators and small testing devices, so-called CO_2 constancy tests (available in pet stores). These devices are filled with tracing fluid that reacts to any changes in the pH of the water caused by an increase

or decrease in the CO_2 content.
• Measure the pH and the carbonate hardness, locate the values in the table below, and at the point where the two values intersect find the amount of CO_2 present in the aquarium, expressed in milligrams per quart (L). The darker shaded area shows the CO_2 values that are too high for fish. The table is not applicable if peat filtration is used.
Tip: A planted aquarium requires about 1 gram of CO_2 per 25 gallons (100 L) of water every day. Adjust your CO_2 fertilizing device (diffuser) so that the CO_2 content of your aquarium water is between 10 and 40 milligrams per quart (L).

Determination of the CO_2 Content in Your Aquarium Water

°dCH	pH 6.0	6.4	6.8	7.2	7.6	8.0
1	30	11	4.5	2.0	1.0	0.5
2	59	24	9.5	3.5	1.5	0.5
3	87	35	14.0	5.5	2.0	1.0
4	118	47	18.5	7.5	3.0	1.0
5	147	59	23.0	9.5	3.5	1.5
6	177	71	28.0	11.0	4.5	2.0
8	240	94	37.0	15.0	6.0	2.5
10	300	118	47.0	18.5	7.5	3.0
15	440	176	70.0	28.0	11.0	4.5
20	590	240	94.0	37.0	14.5	6.0

• The dark shaded area indicates the CO_2 values that are too high for fish.

• Table not applicable if peat filtration is used. CO_2 values = milligrams/quart.

• **How to use the table:** Measure the pH and the carbonate hardness, locate the values in the table, and at the point where they intersect you will find the CO_2 content of your aquarium water. If the values you obtained when measuring the pH and the carbonate hardness differ from those shown in the table, use the values nearest to them.

Alternanthera reineckii *makes an intriguing contrast with the* Hygrophila difformis *in the background.*

CO$_2$ Deficiency

When CO$_2$ is deficient, the plants are unable to assimilate and therefore also unable to produce oxygen. This state of affairs has negative consequences for the aquarium environment. Even if the plants are well fed and well lit, they will grow poorly if there is a deficiency of CO$_2$.

Care: I recommend fertilizing the plants with carbon dioxide. Various methods have been developed for supplying aquariums with CO$_2$:

• Even simple devices, such as diffusion bells with spray bottles, can stimulate growth in your plants.

• Even more convenient are the CO$_2$ fertilizing devices that continually release tiny amounts of CO$_2$ from a pressurized bottle into the water through a diffuser. The amount discharged is kept at a constant level by means of an electronic control device. The pressurized bottles should be replaced as soon as they are empty.

• For short-term use, an organic carbon dioxide device can be employed. It produces CO_2 by means of yeast fermentation. Such device will function for four weeks at most. **Tip:** At night the plants only respire and do not assimilate, so they need no additional CO_2. Consequently you should connect the fertilizing device to the timer switch that also controls the fluorescent lights. It will turn off the device as soon as the light goes out.

CO_2 Surplus

High concentrations of CO_2 will damage only a few plant species, but will certainly kill the fish.

Care: CO_2 can be easily expelled if the water is in vigorous motion, but rapidly agitated water, possibly even aerated by airstones, does not provide the plants with good living conditions because their most important nutrient, the CO_2, will escape. For fish, however, moving water is advantageous. You will have to bear these differing requirements in mind when you decide on the plantings and fish population and shop for the filter equipment.

Water Hardness

Aquarium water may be hard or soft. The hardening constituents are the salts of the alkaline-earth metals, principally those of calcium and magnesium. Water that contains many of these mineral salts is referred to as hard; water that contains small amounts is termed soft.

Aquarists express the hardness of the water in degrees of hardness:
• 1° dH corresponds to 10 milli-

grams of calcium oxide or magnesium oxide in 1 quart (1 L) of water.

Water chemistry uses the concept of the sum of the alkaline earths and measures in moles (gram molecules) per cubic meter or in millimoles (mmol) per liter.
• 1 mole = the weight in grams per liter divided by the molecular weight of the substance in question (1 millimole = one thousandth of a mole). Where the total hardness is concerned, 1 millimole per liter corresponds to 5.7 dH.

Degrees of Water Hardness
The following all-inclusive categories are in common use:

0° to 4°	dh	= very soft water
5° to 8°	dh	= soft water
9° to 12°	dh	= medium-hard water
13° to 18°	dh	= hard water
over 18°	dh	= very hard water

Conversion	
°dCH into	mmol
1°	0.36
2°	0.71
3°	1.07
4°	1.43
5°	1.79
6°	2.14
7°	2.50
8°	2.86
9°	3.21
10°	3.75
11°	3.93
12°	4.29
13°	4.64
14°	5.00
15°	5.36
16°	5.71
17°	6.07
18°	6.43
19°	6.79
20°	7.14

Carbonate hardness: For plants, total hardness is far less important than carbonate hardness (°dCH), which is known as acid capacity and is also measured in millimoles per liter (mmol): 1 millimole per liter = 2.7° dCH.

Carbonate hardness is produced by hydrogen carbonates and carbonates—that is, by the calcium salts and magnesium salts of carbonic acid (see page 15).

Noncarbonate hardness is the term used for the permanent hardness of water which remains after boiling and is produced by calcium sulfate, magnesium sulfate, and other compounds.
• The sum of the carbonate and the

noncarbonate hardness is, as a rule, the total hardness.

Proper water hardness: Most fish and plants do best with:
• a total hardness of 8° to 16° dH.
• a carbonate hardness between 3° and 10° dCH. Only a few plants need softer water—for example, *Aponogeton rigidifolius.* For them—and for breeding many tropical fish—the water needs to be softened.

Measuring water hardness: Test kits and measuring devices for determining the hardness (dH and dCH) are available in pet stores.

Softening and hardening: You can soften the water by either ion exchange (see Glossary, page 58) or by reverse osmosis (see Glossary, page 59). After ion exchange or reverse osmosis, the water will contain almost no salts at all, and it will no longer be fit for either plants or animals to live in. It has to be slightly salinized once more. To do so, add untreated tap water until the hardness is in line with the needs of the plants and animals that you intend to keep (for example, about 2° dH and 8° dCH for *Aponogeton rigidifolius*).

High carbonate hardness by itself can also be lowered by CO_2 fertilization or peat filtration.

The pH Value
The pH value indicates the degree of acidity of the water. All natural water contains a certain amount of dissolved substances that react either as acids or as alkalis (bases). If the water contains more acids than bases, it is said to be acidic; if it contains more bases than acids, it is alkaline. If acids and bases are present in equal amounts, the water is said to be chemically neutral.

Measuring and changing the pH: In many places tap water has pH values of 6.5 to 7.2. Given these values, most aquarium plants can be grown without difficulty. Measure the pH regularly (about every 14 days) with a drop indicator or a pH measuring kit (pet stores).

The pH Scale
The pH scale extends from 1 to 14.
pH value   7 = neutral water
pH value below 7 = acidic water
pH value above 7 = alkaline water
• The further the pH moves away from 7, the more acidic or alkaline the water becomes.
Tip: Most tropical waters are slightly acidic, so tropical plants and fish can easily tolerate pH values of about 5.8 to 7.0.

• If the pH fluctuates more widely (see Biogenic decalcification, page 55), you need to fertilize with CO_2 or make a partial water change.
• If your aquarium contains fish that come from dark bodies of water and plants that do not need a great deal of light, you can use peat preparations to acidify the water.

Carbonate Hardness, pH, and Plants
The carbonate hardness is often subject to wide fluctuations in an aquarium because of the photosynthetic activity of the plants, which affects the pH value.

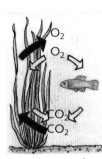

Interchange of oxygen and carbon dioxide between fish and plant. By day: The fish and the plant inhale oxygen (O_2) and exhale carbon dioxide (CO_2). During photosynthesis the plant takes in CO_2 and produces O_2.

If plants are suffering and starving because CO_2 is in short supply, many of them are capable of extracting CO_2 from the hardening constituents of the water (see Glossary, Biogenic decalcification, page 55). They simply split off the hydrogen carbonates and the carbonates (that is, the calcium salts and magnesium salts of the carbonic acid). When this happens, however, the pH of the water rises one to two steps; that is, the water becomes 10 to 100 times as alkaline as it was previously. As a result, the fish are seriously harmed and may die.

This process becomes dangerous primarily in aquariums that are planted exclusively with waterweed and *Vallisneria* species, because these plants are the quickest to decalcify the water.

Care: Wide fluctuations in the water hardness and pH over the course of a day do not agree with the plants, quite apart from the danger to the fish. A well-balanced mix of plants and regular fertilization with iron will prevent serious disturbances. In addition, you ought to fertilize with CO_2, so that the plants have no need to draw on the hardening constituents.

Tip: The level of carbonate hardness is far more important for plant growth than the level of noncarbonate hardness. For this reason, only the carbonate hardness (dCH) is given in the plant profiles (see pages 62 to 89).

Nitrogen Compounds

Nitrogen is one of the most important plant nutrients. Water plants do not absorb nitrogen in its elemental (uncombined) gaseous state, nor do they take it in as nitrate, as land plants do; rather, they take it in as ammonium. Ammonium exists only in acidic water. In the normally slightly acidic environment of our aquariums, ammonium is unlikely to harm the fish, but in alkaline water it changes into poisonous ammonia. Ammonium and ammonia are converted by the filter bacteria first to highly toxic nitrite and then to relatively harmless nitrate. In this process oxygen is consumed. When plants lack the right conditions—for example, in an overpopulated tank with a neglected filter—they are unable to assimilate and cannot produce oxygen. Then the breakdown of the nitrogen compounds either takes too long or does not take place at all. As a result, the fish may die of ammonia or nitrite poisoning.

Measuring nitrogen compounds: The concentration of the various nitrogen compounds is measured with commercially available test kits.

Care: Put plenty of plants, but not too many fish in the tank. Also:
• Take good care of the filter, and change a portion of the water on a regular basis.
• Add fertilizer regularly, because in water with a high oxygen content the ammonium is rapidly extracted from the plants and converted to nitrate. Commercially available fertilizers for aquatic plants contain enough ammonium to nourish the plants properly and to remedy any ammonium deficiency quickly.
Tip: Nitrogenous waste products

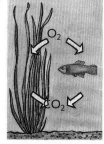

By night: The fish and the plant consume oxygen (O_2) and produce carbon dioxide (CO_2). Photosynthesis is not possible in the dark.

are hard to deal with. As a rule, only a radical improvement of the aquarium environment will help.

Phosphorus

Phosphorus is a problematic plant nutrient. The plants absorb it not as a pure element, but as phosphate.

Phosphate deficiency theoretically would impede photosynthesis and thus also hinder the production of oxygen. In an aquarium, however, this does not occur, because the plants can absorb even minute traces and make use of them.

Phosphate excess, however, which can easily result from the presence of uneaten fish food, leads to plant damage and to heavy algae growth.

Care: By changing part of the water regularly, at least a portion of these waste products is removed.

Potassium and Sodium

Potassium and sodium are present only in very small amounts in our tap water. The sodium content is usually sufficient for the needs of tropical plants, but potassium is in short supply in many aquariums.

Potassium deficiency impedes photosynthesis and thus affects the entire aquarium environment.

Care: Fertilize. Good fertilizers contain plenty of potassium.

Trace Elements

Iron is the most important trace element for aquarium plants. It is a component of the enzymes that help in the synthesis of chlorophyll.

Iron deficiency results in chlorosis (see page 50). In their natural habi-

Flower of Hygrophila corymbosa. *This stem plant, which grows about 24 inches (60 cm) tall, is especially useful in planting high tanks.*

tat, many water plants grow in places where groundwater with a high iron content and other trace elements, such as manganese, copper, zinc, tin, boron, and molybdenum, leaks from the sides of the banks or from the bottom of a body of water in a form that can be easily absorbed by the plants. If the trace elements enter oxygen-rich running water, however, they combine with the oxygen and precipitate—that is, they become insoluble and are no longer available to the plants.

Care: Fertilize. Iron and the other trace elements are already included in most aquatic plant fertilizers. Precipitation is avoided because the iron and trace elements are bound with synthetic organic acids.

• Using iron-rich slow-release fertilizer in the bottom material creates conditions like those on the bottom of tropical waters at the sources of seepage.

• You also can fertilize daily with a few drops of a trace-element complex (follow the manufacturer's directions for use).

Tip: The preparations for iron fertilization and the test kits with reagents for measuring are available in pet stores.

Plant aquarium with neon tetras. Left foreground: Cabomba caroliniana; right foreground: Echinodorus horemanni; behind them: Ceratopteris thalictroides.

Aquarium Accessories

When you are outfitting your aquarium, make the needs of the fish, rather than those of the plants, your prime consideration. Animals have a far more sensitive reaction to overly cold or dirty water than do plants. Nonetheless, plants do have some special requirements, especially in regard to lighting.

Aquarium accessories—including lights, heaters, and filters—make it possible to create optimal living conditions for fish and plants. The light in particular plays the most crucial role where the plants are concerned. They need light as a source of energy in order to sustain their metabolic processes.

Lighting

Light is the most important prerequisite for good plant growth. Plants need light as a source of energy to sustain their metabolism. Because most aquarium plants are tropical plants, they will not thrive in natural daylight in this country. In summer it is too bright and too warm so that too many algae develop. In winter the light is too weak, and the plants become stunted. For these reasons, artificial lighting is essential.

Period of exposure to light: In equatorial or subtropical areas, where our aquarium plants originate, the day is between 12 and 14 hours long all year round. In aquariums these plants also need a day of this length. Therefore you need to connect the aquarium lights to a timer switch.

Light intensity: Plants adapted to the light conditions of their native habitat over millions of years. Many tropical plants, particularly the red-leaved species, are extremely light-loving. Others, however—many *Cryptocoryne* species, for example—will also flourish in shade.

• For fluorescent lights with a daylight spectrum, the rule of thumb is about 1 watt for every 2 quarts (2 L) of water.

• Energy-efficient lamps have a higher light output. Spiral fluorescent tubes are substantially brighter than straight ones, and the luminosity of Lumilux tubes is about 30 percent greater. For these lamps, 0.3 watts per quart (L) of water is sufficient. (The same is true for mercury-vapor lamps, although with them there is no energy saving.)

Important: The deeper light penetrates into water, the more it diminishes. If the large background plants in a tank with water more than 16 inches (40 cm) deep are thriving, while small plants in the foreground are becoming stunted, you should choose types of tubes that are more luminous. Alternatively, install an additional fluorescent light. The same is true for water that has been acidified with peat preparations. The brown color causes the water to absorb a great deal of light.

Light color: Fish and plants look most natural when they are illuminated by a light that resembles normal daylight. When buying lamps, ask your pet-store dealer for advice. Photosynthesis is most intense in the long-wave red and short-wave blue spectral regions. If you are using the violet Grolux or Fluora tubes to stimulate plant growth, you need to combine them with daylight tubes to avoid unnatural-looking colors in the aquarium.

Fluorescent Tubes and Lamps

Fluorescent tubes are the ones most commonly used. The most economical type of lamp, they illuminate the entire tank evenly. Usually they are mounted directly inside the aquarium hood. Alternatively, they may be housed in a special box or installed as hanging lamps.

Changing the tubes: Fluorescent tubes lose their efficiency slowly but steadily. With normal use—12 to 14 hours per day—they retain only 50 percent of their luminous power after six months. I recommend replacing the lights every six months (especially important with violet Grolux and Fluora tubes).

Tip: A high nitrate content increases the light requirement of the plants. In clean water they will thrive with less light, but in water heavily loaded with nitrate, plant growth will stagnate even with an ideal level of light.

Mercury vapor lamps: Mercury-vapor high-pressure lamps can be used above aquariums with water up to about 24 inches (60 cm) deep. They also are suitable for use as spotlights, to directly illuminate plants that need a great deal of light.

Halogen lamps: Halogen metal-vapor lamps have a higher light yield than mercury-vapor lamps and consume less energy. They have not proved especially successful for use in freshwater aquariums.

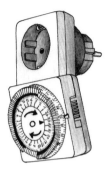

An automatic timer switch, to which the aquarium lights are connected, regulates the length of the lighting period.

Safety in the Aquarium Area

Water damage and insurance: The nightmare of many aquarists—that their aquarium will break—seldom becomes reality. Nevertheless, you should be prepared for such an eventuality and, even before you buy your aquarium, try to have it added to your insurance policy. Ask your insurance agent what expenses will be covered in case of damage.

Avoiding electrical accidents: It is well known that electrical current in combination with water is dangerous. For this reason, it is essential to keep in mind the following safety precautions:
• When you buy electrical appliances, make sure that they carry the UL approval notice.
• Equipment used inside the aquarium has to bear a notation that it is suitable for this purpose.
• Buy a so-called fault-current breaker, available in pet stores and electrical supply stores. Attached between the current source and the appliance, it will interrupt the supply of current immediately if any failure occurs in the appliance or the wiring.
• Before you do any work in the aquarium, pull the plug or remove electrical appliances from the aquarium.
• If repairs are necessary, let a professional do them.

The neon tetras really glow against the rich colors of the plants that provide a backdrop for them. In the foreground, on the right: A small *Cryptocoryne species;* on the left: *Echinodorus osiris* used as a solitary plant; in the middle: various swordplant species; in the background, on the right: *Rotala macrandra*; on the left: *Ammannia gracilis.*

Aquariums in which you want plants of absolute beauty to flourish should be stocked only with small, not overly lively species of fish. You also should not use fish that eat plants or like to burrow in the bottom material. Highly suitable for aquariums are small and medium-sized characins, barbs and small barbs, and all species of live-bearing toothed carp.

Fertilizing with CO_2 and choosing the proper lighting are not the only ways to stimulate the plants to lush growth. By skillfully choosing the heater and filter, you can also successfully promote plant growth.

Aquarium Heating

Most aquarium plants thrive in a temperature range of 70° to 86°F (21°–30°C), but they grow best at approximately 73° to 81°F (23°–27°C). Plants from subtropical regions can also tolerate cooler water. The most adaptable are cosmopolites like crystalwort (*Riccia fluitans*), which grows at tem-

1. *Automatic heater. The adjusting screw has to be above water level.*

peratures from 54° to over 86°F (12°–30°C). Because neither the plants nor the fish can tolerate sudden, sizable fluctuations in temperature, the aquarium heater has to be monitored and controlled by a thermostat. The thermostat will keep the chosen temperature at a constant level, plus or minus about 1.8°F (1°C).

Automatic Heaters
Drawing 1
Heaters with automatic control are rod-type heaters with built-in thermostats. This inexpensive heating device is attached in the aquarium by means of suction cups, so that the cap with the adjusting screw is above the water level.

Thermofilter
This device, which is practical and easy to operate, is a filter with a built-in heating unit that is regulated by a thermostat. The water is warmed during the filtering process.

Bottom Heater
Drawing 2
Bottom heaters will warm the gravel bottom to 1.8° to 3.6°F (1°–2°C) above the water temperature, thus causing fresh water to circulate continuously through the bottom gravel.

Mode of operation: Drawing 2 shows an example of a heating cable installed in an aquarium. The warmed water rises to the top, which causes colder

water to be sucked down from the upper part of the aquarium. In this way a constant supply of nutrients and fresh water is carried to the roots of the plants. Thus the bottom material does not decay, and bacteria that live there can help the filter bacteria break down any harmful substances. This also keeps the plants from getting "cold feet" if the tank happens to be in a room that is inadequately heated.

Laying the Heating Cable
Lay the cable in coils on the bottom of the tank, and mount it on plastic bars or feet so that it does not touch the glass. The cable is also well suited for use in containers in which plants are being kept emersed for propagation.

Heating Pad
Place the pad outside and directly underneath the aquarium; put some suitable insulating material (styrofoam, for example) on the surface beneath it.

Warning: When using a heating pad, make sure the bottom material is not muddy or too fine-grained! Impermeable bottom material does not allow water to flow through it quickly enough, and the resulting heat that can build up under rocks or other wide decorative materials may cause the tank bottom to split! The glass can also be damaged if a heating pad is too powerful or not properly installed.

Care: Because the bottom, by virtue of the continuous flow of water through it, acts as a filter, it gets dirty and clogged after a time, like any other filter. Then the roots of the plants may be damaged, and the filter bacteria may die. Therefore, clean the bottom once a year.

Tip: Instead of heating the entire bottom with a heating pad, I recommend that you use a low-voltage bottom heater regulated by a dual-circuit thermostat that on cool days will turn on an automatic heater as well.

Heat Intensity
In unheated rooms and in rooms that in winter have little or no heat at times, the aquar-

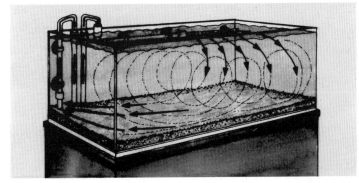

3. *A tank in which plants can flourish needs a cover or hood that closes tightly, gentle water current, and some water agitation.*

ium heater should have an output of 1 watt per quart (L) of water. If the tank is located in a normally heated room, about 0.5 watt per liter (L) is enough.

Filters and Aeration
Aquarium filters remove suspended matter—such as uneaten fish food, loose pieces of plants, and decayed matter—from the water. The filter bacteria convert this waste, along with the fish excreta dissolved in the water, into substances that do not harm the aquarium environment. In so doing, they consume O_2 and give off CO_2.

Important: Because fish are more apt than plants to suffer damage in dirty water, you should give priority to the needs of the fish when you choose a filter.

Tips on Filters and Aeration
Drawing 3
Your choice of an inside or outside filter, and the type of filter

substrate you choose will have little effect on your plants. It is crucial, however, that the plant nutrient CO_2 should not be expelled from the water before it can be of benefit to the plants. For this reason, a tank in which you want plants to enjoy vigorous growth needs a cover that can be tightly closed. Moreover, the water current should be gentle.

Unsuitable for plant aquariums are all pieces of equipment that enrich the water with O_2 and/or cause the CO_2 to escape, for example:
• Filters whose discharge causes heavy turbulence at the surface of the water.
• Outside filters with nozzle tubes as the discharge, through which the water is sprayed back into the aquarium.
• Airstones, which create air bubbles.
• Trickle filters, because the filtered water contains almost no CO_2.

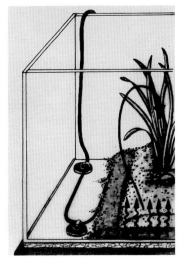

2. *Lay the cable for the bottom heater in coils.*

Choosing and Setting the Right Plants

Because the plants are intended not only to have a decorative effect, but also to be a vital component of the underwater realm of the aquarium, you need to know and pay attention to several basic rules, tips, and tricks when it is time for choosing and setting plants.

Cabomba aquatica *rarely flowers in an aquarium. It is difficult to grow because it is extremely demanding in terms of water quality, and it requires a great deal of light.*

Basic Rules for Choosing Plants

The biological community: So that plants and fish feel equally comfortable, keep the following in mind:

• All plant species should have approximately the same requirements in regard to water composition, temperature, and light intensity.

• Where care is concerned, the needs of the plants should be compatible with the needs of the fish.

Tank size: Find out how large the plants will grow (see plant descriptions, page 64). You will derive little pleasure from plants that you have to keep cutting back to make them fit the dimensions of the aquarium. Plants achieve their true beauty and develop their detoxifying and oxygen-producing properties only if they can grow undisturbed for a long while and do not have to keep forming new roots or healing injuries. For example, stem plants that are cut back and replanted every few weeks become weaker each time and finally succumb. Therefore:

• Tall stem plants like *Cabomba* (fanwort), the large *Hygrophila*

species, and *Heteranthera zosterifolia* (mud plantain) are inappropriate for shallow tanks.

• Do not put plants that grow very large, such as *Echinodorus cordifolius* (swordplant with heart-shaped leaves), in small aquariums—that is, less than 39 inches (1 m) long.

• In larger aquariums, on the other hand, the plants ought not to be too small. A tank 79 inches (2 m) long and 27 inches (70 cm) high will not look very attractive if it is planted only with plants that stay small—such as *Echinodorus tenellus* (pygmy-chain swordplant), *Samolus parviflorus* (underwater rose)—or with low *Cryptocoryne* species.

Arrangement: Large-leaved plants make a nice contrast with finely pinnate ones, light green ones with dark green or red ones, and rosette plants with stem plants.

Unsuitable for aquariums: Houseplants that are alleged to be suitable as aquarium plants—for example, "underwater bromeliads" or "underwater palms"—will vegetate in the water for awhile, do nothing for the aquarium environment, and finally die. The dying plants are a dangerous source of decay.

Tip: The descriptions and photos of 49 attractive aquarium plants (see pages 62–89) will help you make the right choices when you buy plants.

The environmental needs of plants and fish need to be compatible.

Tips for Newly Set-Up Aquariums

When setting up a new aquarium it is best to plant undemanding plants at first. The demanding ones often need a relatively long time to become acclimated and to strike root. During this time, they contribute nothing toward the improvement of the water, and algae have a chance to develop in profusion. Then if the algae plague becomes too severe, sensitive plants die.

Fast-growing, undemanding plants, on the other hand—*Lud-wigia* or *Sagittaria* species, for example—take root so quickly that the algae scarcely have a chance. Later, after the aquarium has been "broken in" for a few months and the plants and fish are healthy, you can gradually replace the undemanding plants with demanding ones like *Cryptocoryne* species and *Cabomba*. If you add a new plant group to your aquarium every two to four weeks, there will always be so many rooted, vigorous plants in the tank that the new arrivals suffering from

In the photo:
An aquarium with lush plantings. Foreground right: A dwarf Crypto-coryne; *foreground center:* Cabomba carolini-ana; *middle:* Cryptocoryne wendtii; *middle left:* Microsorium pteropus.

25

Grasslike plants for the foreground are often sold in tiny latticework baskets. The little basket has to be removed before you can set the plant.

the stress of being transplanted are not needed for water improvement. They also will strike root better in a "broken-in" aquarium environment. **Tip:** *Cryptocoryne* species often will not grow at all in newly set-up tanks!

To prevent algae, immediately place several algae-eating fish in the newly set-up tank (do not feed them for the first two weeks). Otherwise, the algae will grow much faster than the plants. *Crossocheilus siamensis* and bristle-mouth, or blue-chin, catfish (*Ancistrus dolichopterus*) will do the best job, but many other sucker-mouth catfish (*Otocinclus, Panaque, Hypostomus, Rineloricaria,* and *Farlowella* species) and all live-bearing toothed carp are also good algae cleaners.

Why Scientific Names Are Important

As an aquarist, you won't be able to get by without the scientific names of plants and fish. With the great variety of species available, you will be able to avoid making a wrong purchase if you can give the scientific name precisely.

The first name indicates the genus to which the plant belongs.

The second name designates the species within the genus. For example: *Echinodorus tenellus* (little barhead). *Echinodorus* is the genus name, *tenellus,* the species name.

Checklist for Buying Plants

You will find a large selection of aquarium plants in aquarium stores and pet stores.

Usually the plants offered for sale there are potted in small plant con-

tainers. Cuttings are sold in bunches and with their stems packed in expanded plastic or rock wool. Buy only plants that are healthy and—if possible—young.

Healthy plants have firm leaves and stems and a bright color. Plants with many bent or brown leaves will recover quickly with good care if their cotyledons are still healthy, but they are not recommended for an aquarium that has been newly set up.

Young plants adapt to the new conditions in your aquarium more easily than old plants, for which the shock of being transplanted is often so great that they lose a portion of their leaves.

Transporting the Plants

For a short trip from the store to your house, it is all right for the dealer to pack the plants in a plastic bag or to wrap undemanding species in newspaper.

Important: Lay the plants in room-temperature water at once!

For a long trip you should bring along a covered pail or a glass jar and transport the plants in water.

In winter, wrap the pails or jars in thick layers of newspaper or pack them in a styrofoam carton.

Care of the Plants Before Setting

Newly purchased plants have to be cleaned before you set them. First, put the plants (still in their plastic containers) in a bowl of tepid water. To keep them from drying out, cover them with a sheet of newspaper, which will absorb water and keep any plant parts that stick out of the water wet. Remove the plants one at a time from the bowl to clean then.

• Remove the container-grown plants carefully from their little plastic pots. Don't try to use force. To keep the roots from being damaged, sometimes you have to cut the container carefully, piece by piece, away from the roots with a pair of sturdy shears.

• Carefully rinse the glass mineral wool or rock wool out of the root system of the stem plants.

Leaves and stems: You will have to cut off dried-out, crushed, and bent plant parts, as well as leaves that are tattered or brown.

Roots: Cut off all the dead roots. Dead roots are brown and limp, healthy ones are pale and firm.

Snail spawn: Snail spawn may be found on many plants from pet stores and on almost all plants from long-established aquariums.

• It is not necessary to remove the balls of spawn if you have fish and only robust plants in your aquarium. Snails make themselves useful in community aquariums by eating leftover fish food and small algae.

• You should remove the snail spawn if you are planning a tank designed primarily or exclusively for plants, in which you want to include some fine-leaved, sensitive species. In that case, carefully scrape the spawn off the plants.

Tip: By all means remove Malayan snails if you have put a slow-release fertilizer (see page 40) beneath the bottom material. In this case it is preferable to scrape all the snail spawn off the newly purchased plants.

Malayan snails are quite difficult to remove from the aquarium later. As they burrow, over time they will mix the slow-release fertilizer with the upper layer of gravel, and the entire bottom will be a mess. Moreover, a fertilizer high in iron can turn the water red.

The Bottom Material
Bottom material that is lime-free is important for water quality.

Suitable bottom material: I recommend quartz gravel in a grain size of 2 to 3 millimeters.

Unsuitable bottom material: Overly fine-grained gravel or sand is too compact and prevents good water circulation causing sewage gas to form. Overly coarse gravel, however, allows too much debris to fall through the spaces between the pebbles, and as a result the bottom

In community tanks, the ram's-horn snail (above) and the Malayan snail (below) are useful helpers. They will eradicate leftover fish food and small algae.

becomes muddy. If you are using a bottom heater, heat will accumulate (see page 22).

Color of the bottom material: The gravel should be brown or colored; light-gray gravel reflects light strongly, which disturbs the fish.

Slow-release fertilizer: For optimum plant growth, place one of the commercially available iron-rich fertilizers under the gravel. Follow the manufacturer's directions. Slow-release fertilizer is necessary because the plants will grow rapidly when they have proper lighting, and they will consume a great many nutrients.

Tip: Arrange the bottom material so that it slopes; it should be lower in the front than in the back of the aquarium. If the tank is large, create terraces, placing the plants that need the most light on the highest terrace, at the back.

Tips for Decorating the Aquarium

The general aquarium literature gives detailed information about decorative materials and their use in aquariums (see Useful Books, page 93). The following are only a few important pointers:

Stones (basalt, granite, lava, Scandinavian slate, and so forth) have to be free from lime! Brown rocks contrast especially well with the plants.

Swamp pine (available in pet stores), which does not rot in an aquarium, should be cleaned and boiled thoroughly before it is put in the tank. The roots have to become completely saturated, so that they do not float to the top.

Hiding places and spawning places are created by piling up roots and rocks to form caves or by using coconut shells that have been boiled clean.

Back and side walls should be decorated, because all animals feel more at ease if their environment is not exposed on all sides. You can fasten painted paper or styrofoam backdrops to the outside walls. Alternatively, inside the aquarium you can make walls out of rock, cork, or polyurethane. Plastic back walls are also available commercially.

Terraces will visually break up the space in the aquarium. Use silicon rubber to glue upright glass strips to the bottom. Then conceal the front of the strips with rocks, swamp pine, or cork (glued on!) to blend well with the back wall. Building blocks for terraces or peat bricks for making walls are available in pet stores. Then, in the various compartments created by the terraces, you can use different kinds of bottom materials for plants with varying requirements.

Roots and Underground Parts of Stems

To store the starch produced during photosynthesis, many plants use tubers, bulbs, or rhizomes.

Aponogeton undulatus

The stem tubers of *Aponogeton* store nutrients for times of need, and the bulb of *Crinum natans* and the root of *Nymphoides aquatica* perform the same function. The roots of floating plants are used for intake of nutrients. In breeding fish, the roots of floating plants are used as a spawning substrate.

Water lettuce

Aponogeton ulvaceus

Crinum natans

Banana plant

As a rule, setting aquarium plants so as to ensure that they take root well is not a problem. With many plants, however, it is important to know a few basic facts. On these How-To pages and on page 32 you will find tips and tricks to help you plant properly.

Planting Tip for Newly Set-Up Tanks

Before you begin setting the plants, fill the completely arranged and decorated aquarium half or two-thirds full of water. In this way you will keep the plants from drying out and suffering any damage while you are putting them in place. To avoid stirring up the bottom material, lay a sheet of newspaper or brown paper in the tank, or put in a large plate. When you add the water, direct the stream onto the paper or the plate.

Tip: Do not set the plants until the water is warmed to at least 72°F (22°C). Cold water is too great a shock for the plants.

Setting Rooted Plants

Drawings 1 and 2

No matter whether you have bought container plants or bare-root plants, proceed as follows when setting rooted stem plants or rosette plants (without a rhizome or tubers):

• With a sharp knife or sharp pair of shears, cut off one-half to two-thirds of the roots. Leave only enough to anchor the plant in the bottom material and keep it from floating to the top. This trimming stimulates the growth of new roots.

• With your finger, poke a hole in the bottom material and insert the plant in it, as deeply as possible.

• From the side, fill the hole with bottom material. As you do so, carefully pull the plant until the crown of the root is barely visible above ground.

Tip: With *Sagittaria* and *Vallisneria* species, you should still be able to see the upper 2 millimeters of the roots after the plants have been set. *Ceratopteris thalictroides* (water sprite, water fern, or oriental fern) will strike root much faster if 1/2 to 1 inch (1 – 2 cm) of the root system is still showing above ground.

Setting Bulbs, Tubers, and Rhizomes

Drawing 3

With aquarium plants that have rhizomes, bulbs, or strong tubers, you can cut off almost all the roots. Until new roots are formed, the plant will live on the reserves deposited in the storage organ.

Caution: Do not injure the storage organ when you cut off the roots!

Setting Bulbs and Tubers

Drawing 3, left

Bulbs or tubers have to be planted so that the point where the leaves sprout is still clearly visible. Only half of the bulb should be covered by the bottom material.

Setting Rhizomes

Drawing 3, center

Because new roots are formed only at the nodes of the rhizomes, the plant has to be set as deeply as possible. The point

1. *Insert rooted plants deep into the planting hole.*

2. *Fill in the planting hole, and carefully pull the plant upward.*

where the leaves sprout, however, must not be buried under the gravel. For this reason, plant rhizomes at an angle so that the largest part is in the ground and the center sticks up above it.

With *Cryptocoryne* rhizomes in particular, you need to be sure they are planted properly; otherwise, these plants will grow poorly.

3. *Set plants with storage organs as follows:*
1. Bulb: About one-half has to be above ground.
2. Rhizome: Plant at an angle.
3. Roots of Nymphoides aquatica: *Carefully set in the bottom material so that only one-quarter of the root is covered.*

Planting Banana Roots
Drawing 3, right
Aquatic banana plants or big floating hearts (*Nymphoides aquatica*) are hard to grow in an aquarium. When planting them, be sure to handle them with the utmost care.

No more than one-fourth of the banana-shaped roots may be set in the ground.

You also can simply lay them on the ground and fasten them carefully with plant clips.

Important: The roots are so sensitive that they can be damaged easily, develop rotten spots, and finally die if you plant them among sharp little pieces of gravel.

Setting Stem Plants
Drawing 4
Stem plants usually are not rooted. Plant them in groups, but be sure to insert each individual stem in its own hole. This will prevent one rotting stem from contaminating the others.

How to Plant:
• Because leaves will rot if they are covered, strip off the leaves of two or, preferably, four stem nodes.
• Plant the stem two or four nodes deep. If set that deep, the plants can produce plenty of roots, because the new roots will arise at the stem nodes.

Fastening Stem Plants with Clips
Although freshly planted stem plants almost never rot, you should use plant clips when dealing with extremely valuable cuttings that you don't want to expose to any risk: Lay the plants singly on the bottom material and fasten each one separately with a glass or plastic plant clip (available in pet stores).

The new roots will find their own way into the ground. This method is likely to succeed, however, only if you have neither lively nor burrowing fish in your aquarium.

4. *Always set stem plants individually, each in its own hole.*

An underwater garden of this kind cannot be allowed to grow wild.

Special Tips and Tricks for Planting

Many plants grow better if you make some allowance for the shape of the root system or the special sensitivity of certain plant species. Here are a few tips and tricks:

Shallow-rooted plants—like *Echinodorus* and *Aponogeton* species—do best when set in wide, shallow depressions in which you can spread out the roots slightly.

Deep-rooted plants—like *Cryptocoryne, Sagittaria,* and *Vallisneria*—should be planted in narrow, deep holes. Be careful not to dig out any of the slow-release fertilizer when you plant.

Small foreground plants—like *Lilaeopsis novae-zelandiae*—that grow thickly matted in their tiny

plastic pots often cannot be separated. Simply loosen the little bales, trim the roots where possible, and plant the entire clump like a single plant.

Aponogeton tubers, which you will have bought during their resting period, have no leaves. For this reason it is quite important to place them in the correct position in the ground. The "eyes," from which the leaves sprout, have to be on the top side when planted; otherwise, the plant will not take root!

Anubias species have such sensitive roots that it is best not to trim them at all. Simply lay the plants on the gravel and anchor the rhizome with a rock or with plant clips. The young roots will find their own way

The plants have to be tended continually.

into the ground. Using plastic cord, you also can tie the plants to a piece of wood or to porous rocks, where they will strike root. *Anubias barteri* var. *nana,* by the way, is not so sensitive.

Fern species like Java fern (*Microsorium pteropus*) and *Bolbitis heudelotii* grow better on swamp pine and lava stones than in the ground. Fasten them to the wood or stone with nylon thread. If after some time they can hold on by means of their roots, the threads may be removed carefully. If you do plant them, do not bury their rhizome in the ground (see drawing, page 31).

Water lilies (*Nuphar* and *Nymphaea*) should simply be laid on the ground and held fast with a rock or a plant clip.

Crinum species are sensitive to pressure and to sharp little stones. For this reason, wrap the bulbs in peat fibers before planting. Do not cover the root base of the bulbs with fibers, so that the roots are not obstructed when they shoot forth once more.

The roots of floating plants should not be cut. Lay the plants side by side on the surface of the water. If they become tangled during the trip home or if the roots are sticking to the upper side of the plant, just plunge the plants in the water a few times. They will untangle themselves and float back to the surface in the right position.

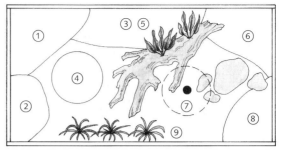

1. *Layout for planting a small aquarium.*

Sample Layout for a 15-Gallon (60 L) Tank

Drawing 1

One root, a few rocks, no terrace, no floating plants (the plants growing from the bottom will bend over at the surface of the water).

The plants:
1. *Hygrophila difformis* (1 bunch)
2. *Myriophyllum aquaticum* (1 bunch)
3. *Vallisneria spiralis* (1 bunch)
4. *Alternanthera reineckii*, red (1 pot)
5. *Microsorium pteropus* (1 bunch)
6. *Ludwigia mullertii* (1 bunch)
7. *Echinodorus cordifolius* (1 "mini" as a solitary plant)
8. *Cryptocoryne affinis* (1 bunch)
9. *Echinodorus tenellus* (3 to 5 pots)

Sample Layout for a 32.5-Gallon (130 L) Tank

Drawing 2

One terrace, one root or several rocks, small terrace wall made of cork or flat stones.

The plants:
1. *Cabomba aquatica* (2 bunches)
2. *Cryptocoryne affinis* (3 pots)
3. *Cryptocoryne wendtii* (3 pots)
4. *Hygrophilia corymbosa* (1 pot)
5. *Anubias barteri "nana"* (3 plants)
6. *Crinum natans* (1 plant)
7. *Vallisneria asiatica* var. *biwaensis* (2 bunches)
8. *Hygrophila polysperma* (1 bunch)
9. *Microsorium pteropus*
10. *Micranthemum micranthemoides* (3 bunches)
11. *Heteranthera zosterifolia* (2 bunches)

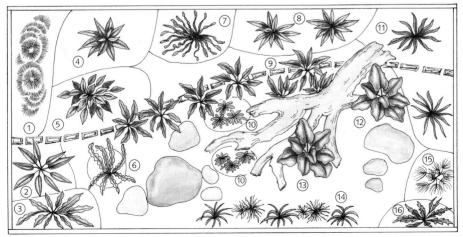

2. *Layout for planting a medium-sized aquarium (52 x 24 inches [130 x 60 cm]).*

12,13. *Nymphaea lotus* (1 plant in each case)
14. *Echinodorus tenellus* (6 to 8 pots)
15. *Myriophyllum aquaticum* (1 bunch)
16. *Bolbitis heudelotii* (2 to 3 plants)

Sample Layout for a 62.5-Gallon (250 L) Tank
Drawing 3
Cover back and side walls with cork, rock, or plastic backdrops. Build terrace of cork, rock, root wood, or plastic.

The plants:
1. *Hygrophila corymbosa* (1 bunch)
2. *Heteranthera zosterifolia* (1 bunch)
3. *Vallisneria spiralis* (1 bunch)
4. *Cryptocoryne pontederiifolia* (2 bunches)
5. *Cryptocoryne willisii* (3 bunches)
6. *Alternanthera reineckii* (3 pots)
7. *Cryptocoryne cordata* (3 bunches)
8. *Nymphaea lotus*, green (3 plants)
9. *Cabomba piauhyensis* (1 bunch)
10. *Limnophila aquatic* (4 pots)
11. *Lobelia cardinalis* (6 pots)
12. *Hemianthus micranthemoides* (5 pots)
13. *Echinodorus tenellus* (about 30 plants)
14. *Hygrophila polysperma* (1 bunch)
15. *Cryptocoryne affinis* (2 bunches)
16. *Vallisneria asiatica* var. *biwaensis* (1 bunch)
17. *Didiplis diandra* (2 bunches)
18. *Hygrophila difformis* (1 or 2 bunches)
19. *Microsorium pteropus* (5 plants)
20. *Hydrocotyle leucocephala* (1 bunch)
21. *Ammannia gracilis* (3 pots)
22. *Cryptocoryne wendtii* (3 bunches)
23. *Nymphaea lotus*, red (1 plant)
24. *Saururus cernuus* (10 pots)
25. *Echinodorus osiris* (3 plants)
26. *Sagittaria subulata* (1 bunch)
27. *Rotala macrandra* (2 bunches)
28. *Aponogeton ulvaceus* (1 pot)
29. *Echinodorus tenellus* (about 30 plants)
30. *Shinnersia rivularis* (1 bunch)
31. *Cabomba aquatica* (1 bunch)
32. *Bacopa caroliniana* (2 bunches)
33. *Cryptocoryne affinis* (3 bunches)

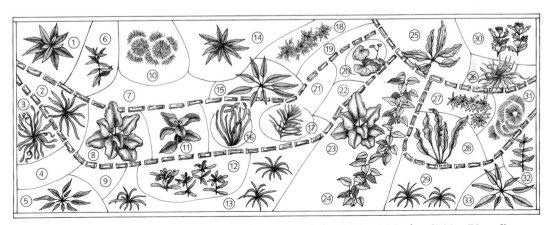

3. *Layout for planting a large aquarium (with an area of about 80 x 28 inches [200 x 70 cm]).*

Flowers of Cryptocoryne pontederiifolia.

In the photos:
Cryptocoryne
pontederiifolia *is a
rosette plant. The
photo on the right
shows the inside
of a flower.*

Setting Up a Dutch Aquarium

A Dutch aquarium is an underwater garden with spectacular plantings. To ensure that the decorative elements and the layout of the garden create an overall impression of harmony, you need to choose plants that have the same requirements for light, temperature, water composition, and fertilizer. In addition, arrange the plants so that their shapes and colors contrast attractively with each other and are mutually complementary in their effect. Even the fish should be chosen to harmonize with the plants.

Tips on Planning and Decoration
You can use stone, wood, cork, and plastic as decorative elements, just as in any other kind of aquarium. Choose whatever plants you like, provided they have the same environmental needs.

Fish for a Dutch Aquarium

The fish for a plant aquarium should be neither too large nor too lively. They also should not eat plants, of course, or burrow in the bottom. These fish are not hard to keep:

• Small to medium-sized characins and relatives of the characins, for example, the cardinal tetra (*Paracheirodon axelrodi*); the black tetra (*Gymnocorymbus ternetzi*); all species of the genus *Hemigrammus*, such as the glowlight tetra (*Hemigrammus erythrozonus*); all species of the genus *Hyphessobrycon*, such as the blood characin (*Hyphessobrycon callistus*); all hatchetfish species, such as *Carnegiella strigata*; all characins of the genera *Nannostomus* and *Nannobrycon*.

• Small and medium-sized barbs that do not pick at plants, for example, the black ruby barb (*Puntius nigrofasciatus*), Cuming's barb (*Barbus cumingi*), the zebra fish of the genera *Danio* and *Brachydanio*, and all small barbs of the genus *Rasbora*.

• All species of the live-bearing toothed carps (*Poeciliidae*), if the water is not too soft (not less than 12° of total hardness) [dH]. Make sure to catch the fry in time and remove them! They will appear in more than ample numbers.

Number of fish: Plan on 1 to 2

gallons (4 – 8 L) of water for each .5 inch (1 cm) of adult fish length.

Maintenance of a Dutch Aquarium

To take proper care of a plant aquarium, you need the following:

• Several hours of available time each week; otherwise, the splendid underwater garden soon will become unsightly.

• An aquarium cover that closes tightly, so that the CO_2 does not escape (see page 11).

• Sufficient light, preferably provided by fluorescent tubes, which illuminate the entire tank evenly.

• A bottom heater (see page 22), because the plants need to grow in a slightly warmed bottom with some gentle circulation of water.

• A filter that does not circulate more than half the water once each hour. The few small fish in the tank do not need more than that, and the plants will stand in water that has only a gentle current—as is desirable.

• If the tap water is hard, the water will need to be demineralized by ion exchange or reverse osmosis, because many aquarium plants (see Profiles, pages 62–89) require soft, slightly acidic water.

• Fertilization with a slow-release fertilizer, which should be placed under the bottom material when the tank is being set up. Then, using liquid fertilizer, feed the plants regularly after every water change. If possible, add trace elements.

Tip: Because plants that have become too large have to be trimmed frequently and the cuttings have to be planted (stem plants in the fore-ground sometimes require this every week), you are constantly in need of new, attractive plants to replace those that are dying off. Most plants cannot tolerate constant trimming and transplanting. For this reason, you should always keep replacements on hand—plants that you raise submersed or emersed in one or more additional aquariums. The most vigorous young plants and new shoots are then set in the plant aquarium as needed.

In the photo: The carpels, which fuse to form an ovary, carry the stigma (yellow), the receptacle for the pollen grains. The stamens perch atop a thin stalk.

Vertical section of a flower of Cryptocoryne pontederiifolia.

Care and Propagation of Plants

Plants need especially conscientious care in an aquarium, otherwise, your underwater garden will quickly be transformed into an underwater primeval forest. That care includes cutting back and thinning out the plants, as well as removing any dead leaves.

Often only a couple of minutes and a few chores are all that is necessary for plant care. These measures are absolutely essential, however, as poorly tended plants not only look ugly, but also deteriorate the entire aquarium environment.

Maintenance Schedule

Aquariums that are set up primarily for keeping plants need the same care as all other kinds of aquariums.

Daily: Check the functioning of the equipment, count the fish, check to see whether they all are healthy, and feed them.

Weekly: Clean the clear glass panes and the hood or cover with a sponge or an algae magnet, remove gnawed-on and dying leaves, and carefully brush off any debris settled on pinnulate plants.

Weekly or every two weeks: Change about one-fifth to one-third of the water. The frequency depends on the number and size of the fish: The more fish you have and the larger they are—or the fewer plants you have—the larger will be the amount of water to be changed and the greater the frequency of change. When you change the water, siphon off the debris from the bottom with the hose, and when you fill the tank, add liquid fertilizer.

Tip: Remove debris carefully but thoroughly from dense groups of

Cryptocoryne species. If the delicate ends of the roots rise up out of the gravel, the bottom material has become too compacted. Loosen it and thin out the plants.

Care of Stem Plants

As soon as stem plants reach the surface of the water, shorten them. If you let them keep growing they will cast too much shade on the bottom-growing plants.

• With plants that branch profusely after being cut back (such as *Hygrophila* species), you can leave the rooted lower portion of the stem in place and let it sprout again.

• Other species (*Cabomba*, for example) branch sparsely after being trimmed, and their new shoots remain small. For this reason, you should remove the entire grouping of plants, cut the upper 8 inches (20 cm) off each shoot to use as a cutting, and plant the group anew, using the tip cuttings and discarding the lower portion.

Care of Rosette Plants

From time to time, remove any old leaves from rosette plants and thin out the groups of plants. Perform all these maintenance procedures very carefully, so that the plants retain their natural growth form.

Plants with large growth habits need to be trimmed. If, for example, swordplants (*Echinodorus cordi-*

folius) or water lilies (*Nymphaea* or *Nuphar*) have grown too large, pick off the largest outer leaves. In addition, using a sharp knife, cut off the roots about 6 inches (15 cm) from the crown of leaves, all around. The plants will then produce new roots, but for the time being will not grow any further. The *Nymphaea* and *Nuphar* species will not put forth any more floating leaves. If you want them to bloom, you will have to leave three to five floating leaves on these plants. If you are not interested in having them bloom, you can pinch off the floating leaves as soon as they appear.

Plants that produce runners: In very dense tufts of plants formed by *Sagittaria* and *Vallisneria* or by mat-forming (cespitose) foreground plants like *Echinodorus tenellus*, large numbers of algae develop in strong light. The fish are unable to eat all of them, and even humans can no longer remove them.

• As a preventive measure, pull out old plants and weaker young plants from time to time so that the plant stock is rejuvenated.

• Because the offsets don't grow singly, but form entire "chains" (see drawing, page 42), you will usually pull out several at once. If this creates excessively large gaps, you can replant some of these plants.

• When pulling out old plants, proceed very carefully. Especially with the small *Echinodorus* species, torn-off parts of roots may remain in the ground, rot, and affect the young plants all around them. Ugly holes in the "mat" would be the result.

• It is often preferable to remove

extremely entangled groupings altogether, pick out the most vigorous young plants, and set them anew (treat *Cryptocoryne* species the same way).

Plants with periods of dormancy: Most *Aponogeton* species, which have a tuber for storage of nutrients, need to observe a resting period. After the plants are set, *Aponogeton* tubers sprout quickly and grow and bloom in great abundance, given favorable conditions. After about eight months they cease to grow and gradually lose all their leaves; they are contracting. When that happens:

• Leave the tuber in the aquarium; after several weeks it usually will put out growth again.

• If no new leaves have appeared after two months, dig up the tuber

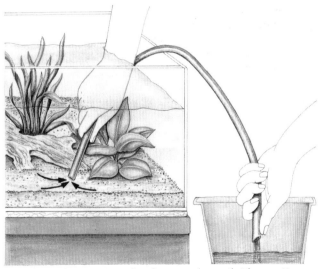

Changing the water with a hose and a pail. The suction of the water flowing out is sufficient to carry uneaten fish food, debris, and algae from the bottom material along with it.

and let it lie on the bottom material for several weeks. It will put out growth again after it is replanted. Do not allow the fish to nibble on the tuber under any circumstances.
Tip: Many *Aponogeton* species are exhausted by the constant warmth of a tropical aquarium and become gradually weaker. Most will do better if you plant them in a shallow clay bowl that you remove from the tank as soon as the plant contracts. Then put the bowl in a cooler aquarium for two to three months. During the period of dormancy the plant can tolerate temperatures up to 61°F (16°C) and less light. Then return it to the tropical tank, where it will sprout again at temperatures above 68°F (20°C).

Lobelia cardinalis *forms brilliant red flowers on aerial stems.*

Feeding the Plants
How often you fertilize your plants and what you feed them depends on the number of plants, the intensity of the light, the water temperature, the species and number of your fish (fish produce fertilizer), and the fertilizer you elected to use. Fertilizers fall into these categories:

Slow-release fertilizers are placed in the bottom material when the aquarium is being set up. Using a liquid fertilizer with iron, add more fertilizer after each partial water change.

Liquid fertilizers can also be used alone in aquariums that have no slow-release fertilizer in the bottom material. Fertilize the first time when you set up the tank, then after each partial change of water. Pay close attention to the manufacturer's

directions, because the dose varies from one product to another.

How to Fertilize Properly
Follow these basic rules when feeding your plants:
• Use only fertilizer products that are designed expressly for aquarium plants! Fertilizers for land plants generally contain nitrates, which will harm plants and fish alike.
• Fertilize moderately but regularly. The aquarium plants will grow better in this way than if they are given larger quantities of fertilizer at long intervals.
• Fertilize after every partial change of water (the amount depends on manufacturer's directions). If you use water-conditioning agents, which precipitate chemicals out of the tap water, fertilize one to two days later.
• Add trace elements daily in minute amounts.

CO_2 Fertilization
Carbon dioxide (CO_2) is the most important fertilizer. Even with ideal lighting and fertilization and properly warmed bottom material, growth will cease if the plants don't get enough CO_2. Especially in tanks with a great many plants, you will need CO_2 fertilization equipment. Install and operate it as the manufacturer directs.

Barbs contentedly share this tank planted primarily with Lobelia cardinalis *(front) and* Heteranthera zosterifolia *(back).*

How-To
Propagation

With aquarium plants, vegetative propagation by division and detachment of young plants is much simpler and more likely to succeed than propagation by sowing seeds.

Offsets
Drawing 1
Plants with a short stem axis (rosette plants such as *Vallisneria* or *Cryptocoryne* species) form runners (lateral branches), at the ends of which young plants develop.

Remember: When propagating these plants don't thin out the offsets too soon! The young plants ought to be at least one-third, preferably one-half, the size of the parent plant (*Cryptocoryne* species, should almost equal the parent plant in size).

With species that put forth large numbers of runners, use only the most vigorous young plants as new sets. Detach offsets, shorten the roots, and set them in a new location (see Planting, page 30).
Tip: Do not detach offsets from floating plants; the connection to the parent plant will deteriorate on its own.

Adventitious Plants
Drawing 2
Adventitious plants develop on various parts of the parent plant. For example, they form:
• in large *Echinodorus* species (*Echinodorus cordifolius* or *Echinodorus bleheri*) on the whorls of the submersed flower stalks;
• in water ferns (*Microsorium pteropus*, *Ceratopteris* species) from buds along the leaf margins;
• in many *Aponogeton* species (*Aponogeton undulatus*) in place of a flower;

2. *Several adventitious plants may develop on various parts of the parent plant.*
Above: Bolbitis
Below: Hygrophila

• in large *Hygrophila* species (*Hygrophila difformis*, *Hygrophila polysperma*) at the point of abscission of individual leaves that have been allowed to float on the water surface.
Remember: Adventitious plants need to have at least eight leaves and strong little roots; young *Aponogeton* plants also need a small tuber.
Do not detach adventitious plants at the pedicels. It is preferable to bend the stalk to the ground and anchor it there with rocks or plant clips. The young plants will strike root on their own.
Tip: Do not detach the adventitious plants of floating ferns.

Cuttings
Drawing 3
Stem plants are propagated by cuttings—that is, by segments of the stem axis—which are

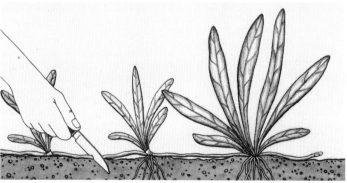

1. *Don't separate offsets too soon. The juvenile plants should be about half the size of the parent plant.*

placed in the ground, where they develop roots at the stem nodes.

Remember: When propagating these plants, use the side branches of stem plants as cuttings. Alternatively, cut the entire plant into a tip cutting and one or more stem cuttings (the lower parts, without vegetative point). Tip cuttings and side branches will strike root quickly. Stem cuttings will develop new lateral shoots that emerge from the leaf axils.

• Do not crush the cuttings when you take them (use a sharp knife)! Each cutting should be 6 to 8 inches (15–20 cm) long and have at least three, preferably more than four, stem nodes.

• Strip off the leaves of the lower stem nodes. If possible, set the cuttings four stem nodes deep in the ground, so that plenty of new roots will form (see Planting, page 30).

Short cuttings, which include only one or two stem nodes, are cut from plants that are not sensitive (*Ludwigia, Hygrophila* species, *Heteranthera zosterifolia*) and inserted in the bottom material at an angle. The cuttings will take root and put out a side shoot from a leaf axil.

Rhizome Division
Drawing 4
The rhizomes (modified stem axes) of *Cryptocoryne* species, *Echinodorus* species, and other plants branch prolifically. At

3. *Cuttings from stem plants: 1. tip cutting; 2. side branch; 3. stem cutting.*

the ends of these lateral shoots there arise young plants that can be detached for the purpose of propagation.

Remember: When dividing these plants the young plants should have about 10 leaves of their own and be about half the size of the parent plant.

• Carefully expose the roots of the parent plant, and with a sharp knife (to avoid crushing)

4. *Expose the roots of the parent plant, and cut off the young plant.*

cut off the rhizome as close as possible to the parent plant.

• Carefully pull out the young plant. Cover the roots of the parent plant with the bottom material again.

• Set the young plant in its new location.

Dividing Older Rhizomes
The older parts of the rhizomes, on which no leaves grow, also can be used for propagation.

Remember: When propagating these plants, dig up the plant. Using a sharp knife, cut off the rhizome about 2 inches (5 cm) from the crown of leaves, and plant the leafed part.

Cut the unleafed part of the rhizome into several pieces. Length of the rhizome pieces:

• *Nymphaea* and *Nuphar* species, 4 inches (10 cm),
• *Echinodorus,* 1 to 2 inches (3–5 cm),
• *Cryptocoryne* species, 2 inches (5 cm).

After dividing the rhizomes, cut off the roots. Place the rhizome pieces in a container of lukewarm water (about 75°F [22°C]). After some time a few buds will begin to appear. Plant as soon as new roots have formed on the rhizome.

Rhizome Division for Ferns
With the ferns *Bolbitis heudelotii* and *Microsorium pteropus,* cut off the back rhizome parts that no longer have leaves but

are still green. The pieces removed should be about 2 inches (5 cm) long. Tie them to wood or rocks, where they soon will strike root.

Dividing Entire Plants
How to divide a large rosette plant:
• With a sharp knife, cut the plant through the middle, dividing the "head," the vegetative point, into two pieces.
• Cut the roots shorter.
• Remove some of the leaves, so that the leaf mass is again in proper proportion to the size of the root ball.
• Plant both pieces.

Preparation of Brood Bulbs
The bulbs of the *Crinum* species form brood bulbs.
Remember: During removal, remove the bulb only when the young plant is about half the size of the parent plant.
• Dig up the parent plant.
• Carefully break off or cut off the brood bulbs.
• Wrap the parent bulbs and brood bulbs in peat fibers and replant them.

Propagation by Seed
Seed propagation is harder and takes longer than vegetative propagation. If the sowing and raising of the young plants is to succeed, you need several aquariums in which to keep and propagate them—aquariums for both submersed and emersed culture. Even so, there is no guarantee of success.

Which Plants Will Flower?
Whether or not aquarium plants bloom depends on the plant species

The propagation of aquarium plants could almost be said to belong to the "advanced school" of aquaristic studies. Aquarium owners need to know not only how the individual plants are propagated, but also how to plant the offsets properly.

and environmental conditions.
In all aquariums, even those with covers, plants that live submersed all year round will flower relatively easily—for example, the water lilies (*Nuphar, Nymphaea*), floating plants like water lettuce (*Pistia stratiotes*), waterweed species (*Egeria, Elodea*), and *Aponogeton* species.
In aquariums without covers, most *Echinodorus* species and almost all stem plants such as *Lobelia* or *Hygrophila* will flower.

Pollination and Sowing
Because natural pollinators (wind and insects) are absent in aquariums, you will have to transfer the pollen from plant to plant yourself.
Pollination: For small, delicate flowers this is done with a fine watercolor brush (marten hair is best), for larger flowers with a cotton swab, and for the largest ones, simply with your finger.
Important: Bisexual flowers cannot be pollinated with their own pollen if the male and the female sex cells mature at different times. Such plants are termed self-sterile. Plants in which the pollen and the ovules mature at the same time usually are self-fertile; that is, they can be pollinated with their own pollen.
Sowing: The seeds have to be collected before they fall into the water and are sucked up by the filter or eaten by the fish.
How to sow: Sow the seeds as quickly as possible after you collect them (the viability of most of the seeds is not known!)

The flowers of Heteranthera zosterifolia *are marvelously beautiful, but rare.*

• Fill a shallow bowl with a mixture of sand and loam.

• Lightly press the seeds into the mixture at intervals of about .5 inch (1 cm) and cover with a thin layer of sand. If the seeds are very tiny, just press them in firmly with your hand.

• Place the seed bowls in a covered aquarium with a shallow water level (up to 1.5 inches [4 cm]). Or, in a large tank, suspend them just under the surface of the water (fasten them to plastic holders or put them on piles of stones). Lower the seed dishes beneath the water, so that the seeds are not swirled out.

• If the seedlings sprout, they will have to be lowered deeper and deeper into the aquarium as their growth progresses. If using an extra tank, you can raise the water level.

What to Do About Diseases and Pests

Incorrect care is often the main cause of stunted growth and plant damage. Only quick action will save the day: Improve the growing conditions of the plants without delay.

If you grow your aquarium plants at optimal light levels and at the proper temperature, supply them with all the necessary nutrients, and do not fail to change part of the water regularly, you are unlikely to see plant diseases or deficiency symptoms. Stunted growth and damaged plants are frequently caused by mistakes in care.

Damage Caused by Fish and Other Animals

Fish and other aquatic animals usually do only a limited amount of damage to plants. Aphids (plant lice), however, can attack emergent parts of plants.

Fish and Snails

They generally cause only minor damage. Fish nibble on young shoots, as well as on the tips and margins of leaves, chiefly those of pinnulate plants. Sometimes snails rasp tiny holes in the middle of the leaves.

Remedy: Healthy, vigorous plants will survive such minor damage.

Insects

Aphids, spider mites, or "whiteflies" may colonize emergent parts of plants.

Cause: Usually the air is too dry.

Remedy: They can be controlled only by mechanical and biological means. Insecticides are poisonous to fish!

• For a mild infestation: Crush aphids and spider mites with your fingers; cut off heavily infested plant parts. Alternatively, feed the aphids to the fish—live-bearing toothed carp in particular love to eat these parasites. Rinse the aphids away by pushing any infested stems and leaves under the water.

• For a severe infestation: Make use of the natural predators of the harmful insects (possible only in covered aquariums!). Aphids, for example, are eaten by ladybugs and lacewing larvae; spider mites by predatory mites. Parasitic fungi may also be used to control insects. Ask for advice in a pet store.

Incorrect Care and Its Consequences

Plants often suffer from deficiency symptoms caused by the wrong choice of aquarium accessories or by their inadequate upkeep.

Insufficient Light

Symptoms: The plants are weak and frail; the leaves are pale green to yellowish; the stems are thin. With rosette plants, there are small leaves on weak stalks. Stem plants have few leaves and long internodes; their growth near the light source is vigorous and compact; the lower portion of the stem is sometimes completely bare. Diatoms appear.

Causes: Use of too few or overly weak lamps, lamps without reflectors, or fluorescent lights that are too old. Too brief a period of light (fewer than 12 hours per day). Algae or calcium deposit on aquarium hood. Too dense a cover of floating plants.

Remedy: Correct lighting.

Wrong Water Temperature
Symptoms: At too high a temperature, stem plants have excessively long internodes and small leaves; there is little growth in rosette plants (symptoms resemble those of light deficiency). If the water is too cold, the plants will cease to grow and after a time will die.

Cause: Too high or too low a temperature; imbalance between warmth and light intensity or between warmth and nutrient supply. The higher the temperature, the faster the plants grow. Then if the light or the nutrient supply is inadequate, growth disturbances will result. In addition, at higher temperatures the plants consume more O_2 and give off more CO_2. In high heat, O_2 consumption through respiration exceeds O_2 liberation through photosynthesis. A deficiency of oxygen in the tank is the result.

Remedy: Check the temperature, light, and nutrient supply and correct whatever is wrong.

Wrong Color of Light
Symptoms and causes: Tall, leggy plants as a result of fluorescent lamps with a very heavy proportion of red in the light spectrum. Low, squat growth caused by a very high proportion of blue. Stunted growth and light deficiency symptoms caused by a lamp with green and yellow light.

Remedy: Proper lighting (see page 18).

Leaves of diseased plants. Left: Serious leaf damage caused by excess nitrate. Right: Leaf showing signs of decay and pierced by holes—damage caused by Cryptocoryne *rot (see page 49).*

Problems in the Bottom Material
Symptoms: Gas bubbles as soon as you poke the bottom with a small stick; stunted plant growth; Malayan snails cease to burrow during the day; the plants are poorly rooted, and the roots start to rot and may turn black.

Causes: The bottom material is compacted or too old.

Remedy: Loosen the bottom material and suction away the debris.

Two days later clean the filter; one week later feed the plants. If the plants have not recovered in two weeks at most, replace the bottom material.

Prevention: Don't leave the bottom material in the aquarium for longer than three years.

Nutritional Disturbances

Mistakes made in supplying the plants with nutrients can lead to considerable plant damage and to massive disturbances of the entire aquarium climate. Such mistakes are to be avoided at all costs.

Oxygen Deficiency

Symptoms: The fish are prone to bouts of disease. With relatively long-term oxygen deficiency, the plants become stunted. Profuse algae growth.

Causes: Insufficient light or nutrients; as a result, the plants are unable to assimilate and thus they produce no oxygen. The breakdown of nitrogen in the aquarium ceases because the bacteria in the filter are working either too slowly or not at all. The consequences are water overloaded with waste products and excess of CO_2.

Remedy: Check the light, filter, fish population, and all other maintenance procedures, then make any corrections necessary.

Carbon Dioxide (CO_2) Deficiency

Symptoms: The plants stay much smaller and grow more slowly than plants fertilized with CO_2. Rough deposits on the leaves (biogenic decalcification).

The black-brush alga belongs to the red algae group.

Causes: A lack of CO_2 can arise even with optimal care, owing to vigorously agitated water or aeration with a diffuser stone, because the CO_2 escapes into the air.

Remedy: Fertilize with CO_2; don't agitate the water so vigorously; don't use a diffuser stone.

Carbon Dioxide (CO_2) Excess

Symptoms: The fish gasp for air at the surface of the water (danger of suffocation, as in nitrite poisoning).

Cause: Oxygen deficiency resulting from incorrect care, overfertilization with CO_2, extremely dirty filters, poor lighting, too many fish.

Remedy: Check the maintenance procedures, adjust the dose of CO_2, turn off the fertilizer equipment at night or connect it to the timer switch for the lights. In community aquariums, make thoroughgoing improvements in the care conditions!

Potassium Deficiency

Symptoms: Yellowing of the margins of young leaves, iron chlorosis (see page 50).

Cause: At the waterworks, potassium is removed from the tap water, hence a potassium deficiency may arise.

Remedy: Regular fertilization.

Phosphate Excess

Symptoms: Production of iron phosphate causes the leaves to turn brown or black and to die. Iron deficiency. If there is in addition a surplus of nitrate, then the algae will reproduce explosively.

Cause: You have neglected to perform the partial water changes.

Echinodorus Osiris *is extremely attractive.*

Remedy: Change part of the water on a regular basis.

Nitrate Excess

Symptoms: A surplus of nitrate—especially when an excess of phosphate is present at the same time—leads to proliferation of algae.

Cause: Too much feeding, dirty filters, failure to change part of water regularly.

Remedy: Perform partial water changes regularly without fail; feed fish less.

Cryptocoryne Disease or *Cryptocoryne* Rot

This is probably also caused by high concentrations of nitrate.

Symptoms: In the beginning, small holes in the leaves or along the leaf margins (like places where fish and snails have nibbled); finally, breakdown of the affected plant or of the entire plant grouping.

Cause: Not yet entirely clear. We do know, however, that unclean water, deficient or improper nourishment (nitrate instead of ammonium), and insufficient light contribute to the development of this disease. Changes in the aquarium environment—for example, a water change after a long time with no change, fertilization after a long period of hunger, changing of a fluorescent tube that is too old for use, or cleaning of a very dirty filter—act as triggers.

Remedy: Immediately improve the aquarium environment. Suction off decaying plant matter. Leave the plants alone; they usually will recover in a few weeks.

Prevention: Regular partial water changes, regular fertilization, prompt replacement of fluorescent tubes.

Deficiency of Trace Elements
A lack of iron, the most important trace element, will cause iron chlorosis.

Symptoms: Yellow leaves that become brittle and glassy and finally disintegrate.

Causes: Too little fertilizer, potassium deficiency, overfertilization with phosphate. In well-fertilized aquariums, also caused by excessively high carbonate or total hardness and pH over 7.

Remedy: Regular use of iron-rich compound fertilizer for aquatic plants or daily addition of trace elements (see page 16). If necessary, lower the carbonate hardness.

Manganese Deficiency
Symptoms: Leaves turn yellow, but the veins remain green.

Cause: Unbalanced fertilization with iron.

Remedy: Use a compound fertilizer for water plants, not iron-rich fertilizer exclusively.

Leaf Damage Due to Chemicals
Symptoms: Algae control agents, fish medicines, and snail poisons can result in leaf damage. The individual plant species react with varying degrees of sensitivity to these factors, and they usually do not react immediately. A few weeks after the use of these substances, however, they will turn yellow or brown.

Remedy: Change part of the water after using any chemical control agent. More than half of the aquarium water may be replaced with fresh water.

Important: Follow the chemical manufacturer's directions.

Leaves of diseased plants. Left: Light-colored leaf veins, yellowish, glassy leaf tissue caused by iron chlorosis. Right: Green leaf veins and yellow leaf tissue caused by manganese deficiency.

Algae Control

It is impossible to keep algae from being carried in. They will be brought into the tank along with newly purchased plants or with water fleas from the garden pond, if not sooner. Newly set-up aquariums in particular are often plagued with algae, but the various algae species can make an appearance in older tanks too. You need to make sure that the algae do not get out of control; if possible, prevent their occurrence in the first place.

Type of Algae	Symptom	Cause	Remedy
Blue-green Algae	Thick, smeary, blue-green, violet, or black-brown coating on the bottom material, rocks, and plants. Water that smells moldy and acrid. Ram's-horn snail	In a newly set-up aquarium, the not yet stable aquarium environment. In older tanks, compacted bottom, too much fish food, overfertilization, death and decay of tubifex in the bottom, poorly maintained filter, tap water loaded with nitrate, infrequent water changes, continuous oxygen deficiency.	Remove coating with your hand or suction it off with the hose, ideally several times a day In older tanks, clean the filter; also change part of the water and suction off debris. Two days later, feed plants to fortify them; to improve water quickly introduce *Sagittaria*, *Egeria*, *Aponogeton*, and *Hygrophila*, which take in nitrogenous waste products. The easiest to use as algae eaters: red ram's-horn snails; the quickest: for every 12.5 gallons (50 L) of water, three Japanese algae bitterlings (*Rhodeus sericeus*). Temperature not to exceed 77° F (25°).
Diatoms	Thin, brown, slightly rough coating on aquarium sides, decorations, and plants.	Insufficient light, oxygen deficiency, excess nitrate.	Intensify light or lengthen daily lighting period. If possible, introduce snails and algae-eating fish.
Red Algae	On plants, wood, and stones, green to blackish dots (black dot algae), threads (beard algae), or small clusters (black brush algae). Beard alga	Carried in by imported plants from Southeast Asia (especially *Cryptocoryne* species), nitrate-rich, hard water with pH over 7 (CO_2 deficiency!). Usually only plants doing poorly are affected.	Red algae are tenacious, so cut off leaves; you can neither suction these algae off nor remove them with your hand without damaging the leaves. Fertilization with iron or CO_2 usually gets rid of them. Also possible is filtration through peat (for at least two months) to lower water hardness and pH. Replace too-old fluorescent tubes. Introduce algae-eaters.
Green Algae	Varies depending on species of green algae. On decorations, plants, and bottom material, cottony deposits (fur algae), dark green dots (green dot algae), branching clusters of threads (green cluster algae), long threads that form a web around the plants (green thread algae), unattached tangles (tangle algae). The microscopically tiny green floating algae of the genus *Volvox* change the water into a cloudy green soup. Green fur alga	Phosphate excess and high nitrate, *Volvox* is sometimes carried in with water fleas, but also occurs in brightly lit tanks and with overfeeding of fish and overfertilization.	With *Volvox*, completely darken aquarium for three to four days. Use an oxydator (enriches water with oxygen). Best to use ultraviolet light, ultraviolet water-clarifier until floating algae have vanished. With a diatom filter (pet store) *Volvox* is easily filtered out. Remove thread algae carefully by hand. To make survival of green algae impossible, lower high phosphate and nitrate content by regularly changing water. Feed fish less. If possible, introduce algae-eating fish.

The plants in a Dutch aquarium are arranged solely according to their decorative value, without regard for their geographic origin. The size, shape, and color of each plant group should contrast with the group next to it and with the other decorative materials.

Aquarium
Glossary

Cross-references are shown in SMALL CAPITAL letters.

A

Acidic
Water with a pH (see pH) of 1 to 7 is acidic.

Adventitious plant
Rooted young plant that develops on a part of the parent plant—in the Java fern (*Microsorium pteropus*), for example, on the leaf margins.

Algae
Lower forms of water plants, without FLOWERS and with a very simple structure, in some cases unicellular. They grow on substrates or float in the water. The following may occur in freshwater aquariums: blue-green algae (not true algae, but closely related to bacteria), diatoms (unicellular), red algae (multicellular), and green algae (unicellular or multicellular).

What causes plagues of algae: Too large a supply of nutrients (NITRATE, PHOSPHATE); that is, dirty water. Too few plants that consume nutrients, too much or too little light.

Remedy: Remove the algae, reduce the supply of nutrients, correct the lighting, put algae-eating fish in the tank.

Important: Chemical agents for algae control can cause severe leaf damage in many plants or even kill them.

Alkaline
Water with a pH of 7 to 14 is alkaline, also known as basic.

Alkaline earths
These are the alkaline-earth metals: calcium, magnesium, barium, and strontium and their mineral salts. Calcium and magnesium combination with carbonic acid yields the salts that constitute the CARBONATE HARDNESS. Their combination with other acids, primarily sulfuric acid, yields the salts that constitute the NONCARBONATE HARDNESS (sulfates). Alkaline-earth salts dissolved in water decompose into IONS. The sum of the alkaline earths constitutes the TOTAL HARDNESS.

Alkalis
The alkali metals potassium, sodium, rubidium, and cesium, in combination with acids, form SALTS just as the alkaline-earth metals do (see ALKALINE EARTHS). Dissolved salts of the alkali metals and alkaline-earth metals make the water alkaline (see pH). High concentrations of alkali salts may change the result when you measure the CARBONATE HARDNESS.

Ammonia
Toxic nitrogenous compound (NH_3) that is produced during the bacterial breakdown of proteins—for example, uneaten fish food, fish excreta, and so forth. It occurs only in ALKALINE water; in ACIDIC water ammonia turns into AMMONIUM.

Ammonium
Almost nontoxic nitrogenous compound (NH_4-) that is produced during the breakdown of proteins in ACIDIC water. In ALKALINE water it changes into toxic AMMONIA. Ammonium, the most important nitrogenous fertilizer for water plants, is essential for the breakdown of plant protein.

Assimilation
"Adaptation, incorporation." In the botanical sense, the term refers to the conversion of substances foreign to an organism into the organism's own substances. In the assimilation of carbon dioxide (see PHOTOSYNTHESIS), the assimilates sugar and starch are created from the carbon dioxide present in the air and water. During this process, OXYGEN is liberated. The assimilates serve to nourish the plants: During internal metabolic processes (respiration, for example), a portion is consumed. When the plant grows, some of the assimilates are converted to cellulose, fibrous

material of which the body of the plant is largely composed. Excess assimilates are stockpiled in storage organs (see BULBS, TUBERS, RHIZOMES) as a reserve for periods of emergency.

B

Bacteria

Minute unicellular organisms. Their cell structures differ sharply from those of algae and higher forms of plants and from those of animals. Bacteria have no true cell nucleus. Some bacteria species cause diseases in fish and plants. Of far greater significance in the aquarium, however, is their role in the breakdown of nitrogenous substances from PROTEIN to NITRATE. Separate species of bacteria are responsible for each step in the process of decomposition. Some of them, in special filters, can even break down nitrate into gaseous NITROGEN.

Bases

Compounds that make water ALKALINE. If water contains more acids than bases, it is ACIDIC; if it contains more bases than acids, it is alkaline.

Biogenic decalcification

When there is a CARBON DIOXIDE (CO_2) deficiency in the water (lack of nutrients) the plants can derive CO_2 from the HARDENING CONSTITUENTS of the CARBONATE HARDNESS. First they decompose the hydrogen carbonates into CO_2 and carbonates. This causes the pH (see pH entry) to rise about one step, and the largely insoluble carbonates precipitate and form rough deposits on leaves and other substrates. Many plants, especially *Vallisneria* species and waterweed, can even destroy the carbonates and obtain CO_2 from them. As a result the water again becomes one step more alkaline.

Biogenic decalcification thus causes the water to become 10 to 100 times more alkaline than it was previously. In the dark, when PHOTOSYNTHESIS is not possible, the process reverses: Carbonates and hydrogen carbonates are formed again, and the pH drops.

Continual fluctuations in the pH, particularly an increase in the pH to a level over 9, harm the fish and sometimes prove fatal to them (alkaline intoxication).

Remedy: Carbon dioxide fertilization. If the plants have enough dissolved CO_2 available in the water, the carbonate hardness and the pH will remain unaffected.

Bulb

Greatly shortened stem (rosette stem) with thickened leaves for storing reserve materials. As with every stem, branching is possible, and in this case it leads to the development of brood bulbs, which may be detached for VEGETATIVE PROPAGATION.

C

Carbohydrates

Primary component of plant organisms. Organic carbon compounds that are formed from CARBON DIOXIDE and water during PHOTOSYNTHESIS—for example, sugar and starch (nutrients and storage materials) and cellulose (for the structure of the plant).

Carbonate hardness

The carbonate hardness is the portion of the TOTAL HARDNESS that is produced by the alkaline-earth salts of carbonic acid. The compounds of the ALKALINE EARTHS with carbonic acid are known as hydrogen carbonates (bicarbonates) and carbonates. Hydrogen carbonates are easily soluble in water, carbonates virtually insoluble. The level of carbonate hardness thus depends on the amount of dissolved hydrogen carbonates.

The level of carbonate hardness affects plant growth to a greater extent than does the level of noncarbonate hardness. Plants can dissolve carbon dioxide out of hydrogen carbonates and carbonates and use it for photosynthesis (see BIOGENIC DECALCIFICATION). Aquarists express the carbonate hardness in degrees of hardness (°dCH), although the newer term "acid capacity," measured in millimoles per liter, is becoming increasingly common.

Carbon dioxide (CO_2)

Colorless, odorless, and tasteless gas that constitutes about 0.03 percent of the atmosphere, it is produced during the respiration of plants and animals and during all combustion processes. The most important plant nutrient, CO_2 is consumed in the course of PHOTOSYNTHESIS. CO_2 dissolves in water and can be expelled by violent agitation of the water, A certain amount of CO_2 is necessary to prevent the HARDENING CONSTITUENTS dissolved in the water from precipitating, that is, from becoming insoluble. The exact amount required is determined by the level of CARBONATE HARDNESS. Planted aquariums need to be fertilized with CO_2 (see CO_2 FERTILIZATION); otherwise, the plants withdraw the necessary CO_2 from the hardening constituents (see BIOGENIC DECALCIFICATION).

Carbonic acid (H_2CO_3)

Water combines with 0.7 percent of the CARBON DIOXIDE dissolved in the water to form the chemical compound carbonic acid. Carbonic acid unites with calcium and magnesium to form carbonates and bicarbonates (hydrogen carbonates), the SALTS that constitute the CARBONATE HARDNESS.

Carpels

Female sex organs. They contain the ovules which become seeds when mature.

Chelators

Synthetic organic acids that enable iron and other trace elements to be absorbed without difficulty by the plants. Chelators are used as vehicles for nutrients in fertilizers designed for water plants. If not enough chelators are present, the oxygen, iron, and trace elements will precipitate. They become insoluble and are no longer available to the plants.

Chlorophyll

Green coloring matter of plants; without it, PHOTOSYNTHESIS would be impossible. Chlorophyll is found in the so-called chloroplasts of the plant cells. In them, the process of PHOTOSYNTHESIS takes place. From light, chlorophyll absorbs energy, which is necessary to set PHOTOSYNTHESIS in motion. Chlorophyll may be covered

by red and brown leaf pigments, so that the color effect on the human eye is altered. The red coloration seen in loosestrife (*Rotala macrandra*), for example, is a result of this. Such plants need large amounts of light, because the red pigments obscure the chlorophyll and filter some of the light.

CO_2 fertilization

Addition of CO_2 (see CARBON DIOXIDE) to planted aquariums in order to stimulate vigorous growth and keep the plants from dissolving the CO_2 out of the HARDENING CONSTITUENTS. The best CO_2 fertilizing devices are CO_2 pressure pumps with pressure-reducing valves and a metering device, the so-called CO_2 diffuser. For the small consumer it is worthwhile to get an organic fertilizing device that produces CO_2 by fermentation of yeast.

Contraction

The shedding of leaves at the onset of the DORMANT PERIOD. Before this occurs, the reserve materials (starch) contained in the LEAF are transported to storage organs (tubers and bulbs, for example) and stockpiled there.

Cryptocoryne disease

Also known as *Cryptocoryne* rot. In the initial stages *Cryptocoryne* leaves develop holes and become glassy, then the plant—possibly even all the *Cryptocoryne* plants in the tank—collapses and disintegrates. The cause is not precisely known; it may be overfertilization with NITRATE. The disease cay be triggered by major changes in the aquarium, such as the replacement of lamps or water changes involving a relatively large quantity of water. Try to keep the aquarium environment on an even keel, and make sure that the water is always clean!

Cuttings
Detached parts of STEM PLANTS; they take root after being planted and produce new plants.

Cutting back
Procedure for reducing the size of plants that have grown too large. With stem plants, it involves shortening the plant, which then usually grows bushier; with rosette plants, it entails removing the outermost leaves and cutting off the tips of the roots.

D

Degree of acidity
Expressed by the pH value. Water with a pH under 7 is ACIDIC; if the pH is over 7, the water is ALKALINE. The pH is measured with an electric pH meter or with the test liquids available in pet stores.

Demineralization
Removal of the salts dissolved in the water by means of ION EXCHANGE or REVERSE OSMOSIS.

Division
Division of the vegetative point into two or more parts for the VEGETATIVE PROPAGATION of ROSETTE PLANTS. Should be followed by a reduction of the number of leaves, because after division the plant cannot nourish all the leaves immediately.

Dormant period
Interruption of growth in an effort to adjust to seasonally determined periods of stress (dryness). *Aponogeton* species need to observe a dormant, or resting, period even in an aquarium. These plants shed their leaves and then, after several months, shoot forth again.

E

Electric conductance
Measurement for the total salt content in the water. Salts dissolve in water, forming electrically charged IONS, which conduct electrical current. The more ions that are present in the water, the greater the amount of current that is conducted. Chemically pure water does not conduct any current at all. Because about 80 percent of the ions present in the water come from the dissolved salts of the HARDENING CONSTITUENTS, aquarists use electric conductance also as a way of measuring the TOTAL HARDNESS.

This value is not very precise, of course, because all the ions, not only those of the hardening constituents, are included, but it is often sufficient for determining the quality of water for aquarists' purposes.

The conductance is determined with an electronic conductance meter and expressed in micro-Siemens per centimeter.

F

Flower
Part of the plant that bears the reproductive organs. These include the STAMENS (male) and the CARPELS (female), which by means of pollen and ovules, produce SEED, which ensures the propagation of the plant (see SEXUAL REPRODUCTION).

G

Gas equilibrium
During gaseous interchange between water and air, a state of equilibrium arises for each gas. If too little gas is dissolved in the water, it diffuses from the air into the water; if too much gas is dissolved in the water, it escapes into the air. The equilibrium value of oxygen, for example, is about 9 milligrams per liter of water.

H

Hardening constituents
SALTS of the ALKALINE EARTH metals function as hardening constituents in aquariums; that is, the degree of WATER HARDNESS depends on the amount of these salts present.

I

Internode
Segment of the STEM AXIS (portion of the stem) between two NODES, each bearing a leaf or leaves.

Ion exchange
In water, the SALTS are present in ion form, that is, as electrically charged particles. Ion exchangers are synthetic resins with a weak electrical charge. They intercept the salt IONS dissolved in the water and exchange them for chemically pure water (hydrogen and hydroxyl ions). Ion-exchange equipment is available in pet stores. There are full deionizers, which remove all the ions dissolved in the water, and partial deionizers, which remove only a portion of them.

Ions
SALTS dissolved in water decompose into ions, that is, into particles with a positive or a negative electrical charge. The amount of ions dissolved in the water determines its total salt content, which is expressed as the ELECTRIC CONDUCTANCE.

Iron
The most important TRACE ELEMENT. Iron deficiency causes chlorosis (a disease in which the leaves become yellow and glassy).

L

Leaf
Organ in which PHOTOSYNTHESIS takes place. Divided into leaf blade (lamina), leaf base, and petiole. On its upper surface (in the case of pinnate-leaved water plants, everywhere), the leaf blade has assimilating tissue in which the chloroplasts are located. They contain the CHLOROPHYLL that is necessary for photosynthesis and that give the leaf its green color. In addition, the leaf has a system of air vessels for gas exchange and buoyancy in the water. It also has conducting tissue, through which the reserve materials (sugar, starch) formed during ASSIMILATION are carried to the storage organs.

Liquid fertilizer
Compound fertilizer in liquid form; it is added to the aquarium after every partial water change, in accordance with the amount of water being replaced.

Lyes
See BASES.

N

Nitrate (NO$_3$)
Only slightly toxic nitrogenous compound, end product of the breakdown of protein in the aquarium filter. Can be utilized by some plants (for example, hornwort) as a fertilizer. Excessively high concentrations of nitrate provide favorable conditions for algae growth; remove nitrate by changing part of the water regularly!

Nitrite (NO$_2$)
Extremely toxic nitrogenous substance that accumulates during the bacterial breakdown of AMMONIUM into NITRATE. Well-maintained filters in oxygen-rich water pass through the "nitrite stage" so quickly that the fish are not harmed. In an oxygen-poor environment the filter works too slowly, and nitrite poisoning is the result!

Nitrogen (N_2)

Colorless, odorless, and tasteless gas. In aquariums it is present in various organic and inorganic compounds that arise during the bacterial breakdown and conversion of proteins. Proteins enter the water by means of fish food and dying plants and animals, and other nitrogenous substances find their way into the water via fish excreta. By the interaction of various kinds of bacteria they all are broken down in many intermediate stages to AMMONIUM/AMMONIA, then through NITRITE to NITRATE (in denitrification filters, even to gaseous elementary nitrogen).

Node

Slightly thickened part of the STEM AXIS on which leaves grow.

Noncarbonate hardness

The portion of TOTAL HARDNESS that is produced not by the alkaline-earth salts of CARBONIC ACID, but by the alkaline-earth salts of other acids, particularly sulfates. The noncarbonate hardness does not disappear during boiling, consequently it is also known as "permanent hardness."

O

Offset

Young plant that arises at the tip of a RUNNER of the parent plant.

Ovaries

The fused CARPELS in the FLOWERS of angiospermous flowering plants. During seed formation the ovaries change into fruits.

Oxygen (O_2)

Colorless, odorless, and tasteless gas; the most widely distributed chemical element. Component (21 percent) of the atmosphere. Indispensable for the respiration of all organisms. O_2 dissolves in water—in cool water better than in warm. In aquariums it is necessary for the health of the fish and permits the rapid breakdown of organic wastes by the filter bacteria.

P

pH

Unit of measurement for the relationship of substances in the water that have an ACIDIC or an ALKALINE (basic) reaction. If acids and alkalis (bases) are present in equal amounts, the water is neutral (pH 7). If more acids than bases are present, it is acidic (pH below 7); if more bases than acids are present, it is alkaline (pH over 7). The farther the pH moves away from 7, the more acidic or alkaline the water becomes.

Photosynthesis

Process in which carbohydrates (sugar and starch) are produced from CARBON DIOXIDE

and water through the action of light on the CHLOROPHYLL of green plants (see ASSIMILATION). OXYGEN is released in this process.

Pollen, pollen grains

These contain the male sex cells. To form SEEDS, the pollen must reach the STIGMA.

Proteins

Nitrogenous organic compounds made up of amino acids. Indispensable building blocks for the structure of all organisms. Many nitrogenous waste products get into the water via the metabolic processes of the animals and the death of animals and plants. These products are decomposed into AMMONIUM, NITRITE, and NITRATE in the filter by various kinds of bacteria that break down nitrogen.

R

Respiration

The process of taking in OXYGEN and giving off CARBON DIOXIDE during consumption of the assimilates for the growth and internal metabolic processes of the plant. Respiration is virtually the reverse of ASSIMILATION, and consequently it is known also as dissimilation.

Reverse osmosis

Procedure for removing all salt developers. Reverse osmosis

equipment (available in pet stores) is attached to the plumbing. With the help of the pressure in the water pipes, the water is forced through a thin plastic membrane that lets the small water IONS pass through, but keeps back the larger salt ions of the HARDENING CONSTITUENTS. Viruses, fungi, and pesticides are also removed to a large extent. Reverse osmosis equipment needs to be in continuous operation.

Rhizome
Thickened underground part of the STEM AXIS. After branching, it produces new plants at the vegetative points, and roots and leaves at the stem nodes. To obtain young plants through VEGETATIVE PROPAGATION, the rhizome, or rootstock, can be divided. Each part will yield a new plant.

Root
Organ that anchors the plant in the ground, absorbs water and nutrient salts, and transports them through conducting tissue to the green parts of the plant. It absorbs assimilates (starches) that have been brought from those parts and stores them. Many species form root tubers as storage organs.

Runner
Lateral shoot of a plant that creeps horizontally over or in the ground. OFFSETS develop on it.

S

Salts
Chemical bonding of metals with acids. For aquarium owners, the salts of the ALKALINE-EARTH metals, which are HARDENING CONSTITUENTS, are of importance.

Seeds
After fertilization, they develop from the ovules located in the CARPELS. They contain the embryos and their nutritive tissue (endosperm).

Sexual reproduction
In flowering plants the FLOWER bears the male STAMENS and the female CARPELS.

Each stamen has an anther, in which the POLLEN GRAINS develop. In them are found the male sex cells. The carpels contain the ovules with the female sex cells. They are often fused to form an OVARY, and their uppermost part, the STIGMA, forms a receiving organ for the pollen grains.

When a pollen grain is transferred to the stigma by an insect or by the wind (pollination), the so-called pollen tube grows downward to reach an ovule in the ovary. In this tube the male sex cells make their way to the female sex cells in the ovules. After fertilization the development of the seed begins, and from the seed arises a plant.

Short cutting
Cutting with one to two leaf NODES and one pair of leaves. Set in the ground at an angle, it will sprout a lateral branch from a leaf axil.

Slow-release fertilizer
Bottom material heavily enriched with IRON and other nutrients. When you are first setting up the tank, place this fertilizer beneath the layer of gravel.

Solitary plant
A large, attractive single plant, usually a rosette plant, used as a focal point in a place in the aquarium that you wish to accentuate (frequently used: *Echinodorus cordifolius, Nymphaea lotus, Barclaya longifolia*).

Stamens
Male sex organs. Each bears a terminal anther, which contains the POLLEN GRAINS with the male sex cells.

Stem axis
The main axis of the plant. It

Limnophila *aquatica* is classified as a stem plant. Once stem plants reach the water surface, you can trim them or allow them to continue to grow floating on the surface. However, floating plants have to be cut back if they take too much light away from the bottom-growing plants.

Limnophila aquatica *is planted in groups.*

Rosette Plants

Aponogeton madagascariensis *is the dream of many aquarium owners.*

The Ornamentals in the Aquarium

Rosette Plants

*The botanical explanation, "plants with a shortened stem axis"
conveys no hint of the beauty of many of the plants in this
category. Many rosette plants are suitable for use as solitary
plants, focal points in the decorative layout of the aquarium.*

*The care and experience de-
manded by lattice plants are
very considerable over the long
run. Among the most important
environmental requirements are
soft and slightly acidic water
(pH 5.5–6.5, 2–3 dCH), not
overly high temperatures (60–
72° F, 20–22° C), abundant
fertilization and peat filtration,
as well as protection against
algae growth.*

Rosette Plants

1 Anubias barteri *has firm, leathery leaves*

2 Aponogeton crispus *has a tuber.*

1 Anubias barteri

Family: Araceae (arum family).
Range: Tropical West Africa.
Appearance: Rosette plant; up to 16 inches (40 cm) tall. Thick, creeping rhizome. Leaves stemmed, firm, leathery.
Varieties: Anubias barteri var. *barteri*—about 10 inches (25 cm) tall, leaves oval-lanceolate; *Anubias barteri* var. *glabra*—about 16 inches (40 cm) tall, leaves lanceolate; *Anubias barteri* var. *nana*—about 4 inches (10 cm) tall, leaves variable, usually pointed and ovate.
Care: When planting, protect the rhizome and roots! Bottom fertilization necessary, well-warmed

bottom and CO_2 fertilization recommended.
Light: 30 watts per 25 gallons (100 L).
Water: 72°–82°F (22°–28°C); 2°–15°dCH; pH 6.0–7.5.
Propagation: By side shoots on the rhizome; rhizome division.
Placement: Use taller-growing varieties as solitary plants or in groups in the center and background, smaller varieties in groups in the foreground.

2 Aponogeton crispus

Family: Aponogetonaceae (water hawthorn family).
Range: Sri Lanka.
Appearance: Rosette plant; up to

20 inches (50 cm) tall. Tuber as food-storage organ. Leaves stemmed, lanceolate to oblong-elliptical; leaf margins extremely undate. Flower whitish, single-spiked, bisexual, self-fertile; puts forth pedicels above water level.
Care: Only submersed culture is possible. Nutrient-rich bottom and fertilizer that contains iron. Remember its dormant period!
Light: 50 watts per 25 gallons (100 L), or more.
Water: 72°–86°F (22°–30°C); 2°–15°dCH; pH 6.0–7.5.
Propagation: By seed; artificial pollination necessary.
Placement: Single plant in center; also in groups in large aquariums.

Rosette Plants

1 Aponogeton rigidifolius *has a rhizome.*

2 Aponogeton ulvaceus *tolerates agitated water well.*

1 Aponogeton rigidifolius

Family: Aponogetonaceae (water hawthorn family).
Range: Sri Lanka.
Appearance: Rosette plant; over 24 inches (60 cm) tall. Rhizome (not a tuber). Leaves stemmed, stiffly erect, slightly brittle, rough, and hard; dark green to olive brown, slightly undate along the margin. Flower single-spiked, greenish, self-sterile.
Care: No dormant period, because there is no tuber to store nutrients. Ultrasensitive—clean water and unfertilized bottom are important; to feed, use iron-rich liquid fertilizer. With CO_2 fertilization the plant will tolerate somewhat harder water. Always has low tolerance for being transplanted.
Light: 50 watts per 25 gallons (100 L).
Water: 72°–82°F (22°–28°C); 1°–3°dCH; pH 5.5–6.5.
Propagation: Side shoots on the rhizome. Extremely difficult to raise seedlings.
Placement: Use singly, ideally in large aquariums.

2 Aponogeton ulvaceus

Family: Aponogetonaceae (water hawthorn family).
Range: Madagascar.
Appearance: Rosette plant; up to 24 inches (60 cm) tall. Round, smooth tuber (see photo, page 29). Leaves stemmed, highly undate and often contorted; light green, almost translucent, reddish if in very bright place. Flower twin-spiked, yellow, self-sterile.
Care: Bottom fertilizer not absolutely necessary, but liquid fertilizer that contains iron is called for. Flourishes well in agitated water. In overly weak light grows very tall and thin. Remember its period of dormancy!
Light: 50 watts per 25 gallons (100 L).
Water: 64°–82°F (18°–28°C); 2°–15°dCH; pH 5.5–7.5.
Propagation: By seed.
Placement: Use singly, ideally in large aquariums.

Rosette Plants

3 Aponogeton undulatus *can easily be propagated by adventitious plants that form on the flower stalk.*

4 Barclaya longifolia *frequently flowers in the aquarium.*

3 Aponogeton undulatus

Family: Aponogetonaceae.
Range: India and Indochina.
Appearance: Rosette plant; about 16 inches (40 cm) tall. Has a tuber (see photo, page 29). Leaves stemmed, light green; leaf margins undate, markedly so if in a bright spot; in poor light the leaves are almost smooth. Formation of flowers is rare; adventitious plant often develops on peduncle.
Care: Iron-rich fertilizer and bottom material relatively rich in nutrients recommended. Remember its dormant periods!
Light: 50 watts per 25 gallons (100 L).
Water: 72°–82°F (22°–28°C);

5°–12°dCH; pH 6.5–7.5.
Propagation: By adventitious plants. Once the adventitious plant has a small tuber, roots, and about five or six leaves, you can remove it and plant it, or bend the peduncle downward and fasten it securely.
Placement: Use singly; also in groups in very large tanks.

4 Barclaya longifolia

Family: Nymphaeceae.
Range: Burma, Thailand, Vietnam.
Appearance: Rosette plant; 10 to 20 inches (25–50 cm) tall. Small rhizome. Leaves stemmed, lanceolate; leaf margins undate, more pronouncedly so in strong light. Frequently blooms in the aquar-

ium. Submersed and emersed flowers remain closed but produce seeds capable of germinating.
Care: Iron-rich fertilizer absolutely essential; fertilization of bottom material and CO_2 fertilization are recommended. Low tolerance for being transplanted; for several weeks thereafter check rhizome for patches of decay. Remove any you find. Red plants need more light than olive-green ones. With excess CO_2, holes appear.
Light: About 50 watts per 25 gallons (100 L).
Water: 72°–82°F (22°–28°C); 2°–12° dCH; pH 6.0–7.0.
Propagation: By seed or side shoots on rhizome.
Placement: Use singly.

Rosette Plants

1 Crinum natans *needs very bright light.*

2 Plant Cryptocoryne affinis *in groups.*

1 *Crinum natans*

Family: Amaryllidaceae (amaryllis family).
Range: Africa.
Appearance: Rosette plant; 20 to 40 inches (50–100 cm) tall. Bulb serves as nutrient storage organ (see photo, page 29). Leaves unstemmed, ligamentous, bright green, and burled; more heavily burled in good light than in shade. Flower is white, rarely forms in aquarium; inflorescence about 32 inches (80 cm) high.
Care: Bright light! Nutrient-rich bottom; stunted growth in hard water. Does not tolerate trypaflavin (contained in some fish medications and algicides).

Light: 50 watts per 25 gallons (100 L); more is better.
Water: 75°–86°F (24°–30°C); 2°–10°dCH; pH 5.5–7.0.
Propagation: By brood bulbs.
Placement: Use singly; in background in large, high aquariums.

2 *Cryptocoryne affinis*
Prolific Cryptocoryne

Family: Araceae (arum family).
Range: Malay Peninsula.
Appearance: Rosette plant; 4 to 12 inches (10–30 cm) tall. Small rhizome. Leaves stemmed; submersed leaves oblong-ovate to broad-lanceolate, slightly burled and undate; upper surface of leaves dark green, underside wine-red. If grown emersed, shorter and smoother leaves, often with flower formation, the standard being violet-black and the throat whitish-green.
Care: Undemanding, tolerates subdued light and relatively hard water. With regular fertilizing (iron), large groups of plants develop. Susceptible to *Cryptocoryne* rot after changes of any kind.
Light: 30 watts per 25 gallons (100 L).
Water: 72°–82°F (22°–28°C); 3°–15°dCH; pH 6.0–7.0.
Propagation: By runners.
Placement: Use in groups; depending on the aquarium size, in the foreground or center.

Rosette Plants

3 Cryptocoryne cordata *is quite demanding.*

4 Cryptocoryne pontederiifolia *forms runners.*

3 *Cryptocoryne cordata*
Trumpet Cryptocoryne

Family: Araceae (arum family).
Range: Malay Peninsula.
Appearance: Rosette plant; up to
20 inches (50 cm) tall. A principal
representative of the *Cryptocoryne
cordata* group. Appearance varies
in accordance with environmental
conditions. Described by many
different names (for example,
*Cryptocoryne blassii, Crypto-
coryne kerrii*). Leaves long-
stemmed, ovate to cordate; upper
surface green, violet-mottled,
violet, or reddish brown; underside
cream-colored, red-brown to
violet. Flowers form in emersed
culture, standard yellow to red-
brown, throat yellow.
Care: Demanding. Nutrient-rich,
well-warmed bottom material;
regular fertilization with iron. Do
not injure roots!
Light: 50 watts per 25 gallons
(100 L).
Water: 75°–82°F (24°–28°C);
2°–8°dCH; pH 5.5–7.0.
Propagation: By runners.
Placement: Use singly or in groups.

4 *Cryptocoryne pontederiifolia*

Family: Araceae (arum family).
Range: Sumatra, Borneo.
Appearance: Rosette plant; about
14 inches (35 cm) tall. Thin rhizome. Leaves stemmed, oval-
lanceolate, slightly burled, green,
underside pale rose in color. Stems
long, brownish. In emersed culture
grows more compact and vigorous
and blooms with regularity.
Care: Nutrient-rich bottom material, fertilizer that contains iron.
Transplant as seldom as possible to
prevent stunted growth. Roots are
sensitive!
Light: About 50 watts per 25
gallons (100 L).
Water: 72°–82°F (22°–28°C);
2°–12°dCH; pH 6.0–7.2.
Propagation: By runners.
Placement: With bright lighting,
use as a solitary plant; it will grow
compact and spread out. In shade
it will grow taller and narrower.
Tip: Sturdy plant, may be used
even with robust fish.

Rosette Plants

2 Cryptocoryne willisii *is a decorative plant for the foreground; it forms dense, light-green mats. With good living conditions it grows rapidly, produces large numbers of runners, and has to be thinned out from time to time.*

1 Cryptocoryne wendtii *regularly produces runners.*

1 *Cryptocoryne wendtii*
Wendt's Cryptocoryne

Family: Araceae (arum family).
Range: Sri Lanka.
Appearance: Rosette plant; 4 to 16 inches (10–40 cm) tall. Many varieties and commercially available forms with green, olive-green, or red-brown leaves that vary in size, shape, and color. Appearance also heavily dependent on light. Flowers form in emersed culture.
Care: Fertilized bottom, iron-rich fertilizer. Regularly thin out groups. Susceptible to *Cryptocoryne* rot if the growing conditions change rapidly.
Light: 50 watts per 25 gallons .

Water: 75°–82°F (24°–28°C); 2°–15°dCH; pH 6.5–7.5.
Propagation: By runners.
Placement: Use as a solitary plant; alternatively, put in groups (in dense groups all varieties will grow taller and narrower), with the small varieties in the foreground and the larger ones in the middle of the tank.

2 *Cryptocoryne willisii*
Willis' Cryptocoryne

Family: Araceae (arum family).
Range: Sri Lanka.
Appearance: Rosette plant; up to 6 inches (15 cm) tall. Leaves stemmed, oblong-oval to lanceo-late, green; stems brownish to green. Produces runners in large numbers. In emersed culture grows more compact and puts forth flowers with violet standards and yellowish to violet throats.
Care: Fertilized bottom material, frequent water changes with regular addition of fertilizer. Thin out the groups from time to time, and keep algae under control.
Light: 50 watts per 25 gallons (100 L).
Water: 72°–86°F (22°–30°C); 2°–15°dCH; pH 6.5–7.5.
Propagation: By runners.
Placement: In foreground, set in groups. The brighter the light, the flatter and broader the plants will be (ground cover); they will form dense ornamental mats.

Rosette Plants

3 Echinodorus amazonicus *grows about 20 inches (50 cm) tall.*

4 Echinodorus bleheri *needs a fertilizer that contains iron.*

3 *Echinodorus amazonicus*
Amazon Sword Plant

Family: Alismataceae.
Range: Brazil.
Appearance: Rosette plant; up to about 20 inches (50 cm) tall. Short rhizome. Leaves narrow-lanceolate, often slightly curved in a scimitar shape (ensiform), green; stems fairly short.
Care: Tolerates soft water better than hard; with high level of carbonate hardness becomes stunted despite good fertilization—then CO_2 fertilization is necessary. Loose bottom material and use of an iron-containing fertilizer are important if this plant is to thrive!

Light: 50 watts per 25 gallons (100 L).
Water: 72°–82°F (22°–28°C); 2°–12°dCH; pH 6.5–7.2.
Propagation: By adventitious plants on the submersed peduncles.
Placement: Use singly; in large aquariums in groups in the background.

4 *Echinodorus bleheri*
Family: Alismataceae.
Range: Tropical South America.
Appearance: Rosette plant; over 20 inches (50 cm) tall. Leaves stemmed, lanceolate, green. The plant resembles *Echinodorus amazonicus* (see left), but has broader leaves.

Care: Tolerates higher levels of carbonate hardness, but absolutely must be fertilized regularly with iron to keep the young, unopened leaf buds from becoming yellow and glassy.
Light: 50 watts per 25 gallons (100 L), but also tolerates less.
Water: 72°–86°F (22°–30°C); 2°–18°dCH; pH 6.5–7.5.
Propagation: By adventitious plants that develop on the peduncle.
Placement: Use singly, in large tanks as group plants in the background.

Rosette Plants

1 Echinodorus cordifolius *is suitable only for large tanks. If the plant is kept in a tank without a cover, it will also flower.*

1 Echinodorus cordifolius
Swordplant or Creeping Burhead

2 Echinodorus horemanni *is quite decorative.*

Family: Alismataceae.
Range: Central and southern North America, Mexico.
Appearance: Rosette plant; over 20 inches (50 cm) tall. Leaves stemmed, cordate, brilliant green. Floating leaves long-stemmed. Flowers (white) in open aquarium.
Care: Remove floating leaves to prevent the plant from shedding the submersed leaves. The floating leaves will also take too much light from the other plants. Abundant fertilization will result in luxuriant growth. In small indoor aquariums, plant in small pots; alternatively, from time to time cut off the roots all the way around. Can also be cut back.

Light: 50 watts per 25 gallons (100 L).
Water: 72°–82°F (22°–28°C); 5°–15°dCH; pH 6.5–7.5.
Propagation: By adventitious plants on the peduncles; sometimes also by seed.
Placement: Use singly in aquariums of 62.5 gallons (250 L) or more; grows best in large, open aquariums.

2 Echinodorus horemanni

Family: Alismataceae.
Range: Southern Brazil.
Appearance: Rosette plant; over 24 inches (60 cm) tall. Leaves short-stemmed, lanceolate, stiff, parchment-like, dark green,

slightly undate along the margins. A red-leaved variety of this ornamental plant is occasionally available commercially.
Care: Tolerates cool water better than warm. Plenty of light, nutrient-rich bottom material, and regular addition of fertilizer (iron) are essential; CO_2 fertilization is advisable.
Light: 50 watts per 25 gallons (100 L).
Water: 64°–79°F (18°–26°C); 2°–15°dCH; pH 6.5–7.5.
Propagation: By side shoots on the rhizome; by adventitious plants on submersed flower shoots.
Placement: Use singly.

Rosette Plants

3 In an aquarium, Echinodorus osiris *produces adventitious plants on the flower stalks. The young leaves and young plants have a reddish hue.*

3 Echinodorus osiris

Family: Alismataceae
Range: Southern Brazil.
Appearance: Rosette plant; about 20 inches (50 cm) tall. Leaves stemmed, lanceolate, slightly undate along the margins, green; young leaves are reddish. In an aquarium produces adventitious plants on the peduncles.
Care: Tolerates hard water; will grow in weak light. In strong light, a nutrient-rich bottom and regular addition of fertilizer (iron) are absolutely essential to keep the plant from becoming stunted; the water then should be no colder than 75°F (24°C).
Light: About 50 watts per 25 gallons (100 L).
Water: 65°–82°F (18°–28°C); 5°–18°dCH; pH 6.5–7.5.
Propagation: By side shoots on the

rhizome, adventitious plants on the peduncle.
Placement: Use singly.

4 Nymphaea lotus
Lotus Lily, Egyptian Water Lily, Egyptian Lily, White Lily

Family: Nymphaeaceae.
Range: East Africa, Madagascar, Southeast Asia.
Appearance: Rosette plant; 10 to 20 inches (25–50 cm) tall. Submersed leaves stemmed, roundish to oval, slightly undate with deeply notched base. Floating leaves very long-stemmed, more or less cordate with a coarsely serrate margin. Flowers yellow-white, fragrant, measuring up to 4

4 *There are many varieties of* Nymphaea lotus

inches (10 cm) across; night-blooming, self-fertile.
Varieties: Nymphaea lotus var. *viridis*—leaves green, spotted with dark red; *Nymphaea lotus* var. *rubra*—leaves red with dark-red spots. Many gradations of color.
Care: If you want the plant to bloom, it will have to retain three to five of the floating leaves; otherwise, pinch them off. Compact growth in good light.
Light: 50 watts per 25 gallons (100 L).
Water: 72°–82°F (22°–28°C); 2°–12°dCH; pH 5.5–7.5.
Propagation: By seedlings; by runners from rhizomes.
Placement: Use singly in large aquariums.

Rosette Plants

1 Nymphoides aquatica *is hard to grow.*

2 Sagittaria subulata *is ideal for beginners.*

1 Nymphoides aquatica
Big Floating Heart, Banana Plant

Family: Menyanthaceae.
Range: USA (Florida).
Appearance: Rosette plant; about 6 inches (15 cm) tall. Submersed leaves long-stemmed, cordate, slightly undate, light green to reddish. Banana-shaped roots store nutrients; floating leaves coarser, olive-green, underside reddish. After floating leaves appear, flowers (white) form. Then the plant produces adventitious plants, but they lack "bananas."
Care: Set the banana-shaped roots so that only one-quarter of their length is covered. Alternatively, just press them in lightly.
Light: 50 watts per 25 gallons (100 L), or more.
Water: 68°–82°F (20°–28°C); 5°–10°dCH; pH 6.5–7.2.
Propagation: Firmly press adventitious plants or fully formed leaves into damp ground.
Placement: Singly in foreground.

2 Sagittaria subulata
Hudson Sagittaria, Ribbon Wapato

Family: Alismataceae.
Range: American East Coast; parts of South America.
Appearance: Up to 24 inches tall. Submersed leaves unstemmed, ligamentous, blunt. Inflorescences white, floating on thin stalks, rise above water level. Fast-growing, forms dense clusters.
Varieties: Leaf width variable. Var. *subulata*—up to 12 inches tall. Var. *gracillima*—24 to 36 inches tall. Var. *kurtziana*—up to 20 inches tall.
Care: Completely undemanding; plants need to be replaced with new ones from time to time.
Light: 50 watts per 25 gallons (100 L), or less.
Water: 68°–82°F (20°–28°C); 2°–15°dCH; pH 6.0–7.8.
Propagation: By runners.
Placement: Use in background.

Rosette Plants

3 Plant Samolus parviflorus *in groups in the foreground.*

4 Vallisneria spiralis.

3 *Samolus parviflorus*
Water Pimpernel

Family: Primulaceae.
Range: North and South America, West Indies.
Appearance: Rosette plant; 4 inches (10 cm) tall. Leaves up to 3 inches (8 cm) long, short-stemmed, spatulate; light green, leaf veins almost white; has white flowers and bears fruit in emersed culture.
Care: Feed well; needs plenty of light. Don't plant too deep!
Light: 75 watts per 25 gallons (100 L).
Water: 64°–75°F (18°–24°C); 5°–12°dCH; pH 6.5–7.5.
Propagation: Only in emersed

culture; by seeds, which germinate rapidly. In optimum conditions, formation of side shoots.
Placement: Foreground, in groups.

4 *Vallisneria spiralis*
Corkscrew Vallisneria

Family: Hydrocharitaceae.
Range: Tropics and subtropics.
Appearance: Rosette plant; over 20 inches (50 cm) tall. Leaves unstemmed, ligamentous, blunt. Whitish flowers at the water surface on spiraling stems.
Care: Undemanding. One of the oldest aquarium plants. Produces runners prolifically, so dense clusters develop quickly. Set in narrow, deep holes when planting.

Light: 50 watts per 25 gallons (100 L).
Water: 59°–86°F (15°–30°C); 5°–12°dCH; pH 6.5–7.5.
Propagation: By runners.
Placement: Use in background and along sides of relatively large aquariums and/or in groups in the central area or in the front corners.
Tip: *Vallisneria gigantea* is also a reliable, robust aquarium plant, but its extremely long leaves make it suitable only for high tanks.

1 Alternanthera reineckii *goes well with finely pinnate, light-green plants.*

Pretty in Groups

Stem Plants

Stem plants form the "green frame" for an underwater garden. They are planted predominantly along the sides and in the center and background. They are easy to propagate.

1 *Alternanthera reineckii* Copperleaf

Family: Amaranthaceae.
Range: Tropical America.
Appearance: Stem plant; about 20 inches (50 cm) tall. Leaves stemmed, decussate, lanceolate; upper sides olive-green to olive-brown or red, undersides red-violet. In emersed culture, small white inflorescences may appear in the leaf axils. Variable species with several forms available commercially; best suited for aquariums is *Alternanthera reineckii*.
Care: Iron-rich fertilizer necessary, nutritient-rich bottom and CO_2 fertilization recommended. With insufficient light and nutrients, the red coloration of leaves will fade and margins will become smooth.
Light: 75 watts per 25 gallons (100 L).
Water: 72°–86°F (22°–30°C); 2°–12°dCH; pH 5.5–7.5.
Propagation: By cuttings; with emersed culture, by seeds. When setting groups of varying heights, proceed with care because of the fragility of the stems; do not plant too close together.
Placement: Use in groups in the foreground or middle. Goes well with pinnulate, light-green plants.
Tip: Planted in groups, copperleaf will add decorative spots of color to the predominantly green aquarium plantings. Make sure that floating plants do not rob it of light, and keep algae from settling on it.

Stem Plants

2 Ammannia gracilis *will become stunted if there is not enough light.*

3 Feed Bacopa caroliniana *with regularity.*

2 Ammannia gracilis

Family: Lythraceae.
Range: Tropical Africa.
Appearance: Stem plant; about 20 inches (50 cm) tall. Leaves sessile, decussate, narrow-lanceolate, olive-green to reddish brown. Flowers small, in groups in leaf axils (see photo, page 94).
Care: If sufficient light and nutrients are not available, etiolation and stunted growth will result. Iron-rich fertilizer necessary if leaves are to maintain their color. If the bottoms of the stalks become bare, place low plants in front of them.
Light: 75 watts per 25 gallons (100 L).
Water: 68°–82°F (20°–28°C); 2°–12°dCH; pH 5.5–7.5.
Propagation: By cuttings; in emersed culture, by seeds; raising seedlings not difficult.
Placement: Use in groups in the middle and background or along the sides. Goes well with green plants.

3 Bacopa caroliniana
Water Hyssop

Family: Scrophulariaceae.
Range: Southern, central USA.
Appearance: Stem plant; about 16 inches (40 cm) tall. Leaves sessile, decussate, elliptical; light green, slightly tinged with reddish color in very strong light. Emersed leaves fleshy with an oily sheen.
Similar species: Bacopa monnieri—up to 10 inches (25 cm) tall, similar needs; *Bacopa rotundifolia*—needs soft water, tolerates submersed culture less well than the other species.
Care: Regular fertilization necessary; with CO_2 fertilization, harder water can be used.
Light: 50 watts per 25 gallons (100 L).
Water: 72°–82°F (22°–28°C); 5°–15°dCH; pH 6.0–7.5.
Propagation: By cuttings.
Placement: Use in groups in the middle and background or along the sides.

Stem Plants

1 Cabomba aquatica *is hard to grow.*

2 Cabomba caroliniana *will not tolerate CO₂ deficiency.*

1 *Cabomba aquatica*
Fanwort

Family: Nymphaeaceae.
Range: Northern South America to southern North America.
Appearance: Stem plant; about 20 inches (50 cm) tall. Leaves stemmed, decussate, very finely pinnate with hundreds of individual segments. Floating leaves and flowers (see photo, page 94) possible.
Care: Hard to grow; needs very clean water, clean bottom, plenty of light, fertilization with iron. Does not tolerate hard or alkaline water. Keep debris and algae growth under control!

Light: 100 watts per 25 gallons (100 L).
Water: 75°–82°F (24°–28°C); 2°–8°dCH; pH 6.0–6.8.
Propagation: By cuttings.
Placement: Middle and background of tall aquariums; set in groups. Goes well with dark and large-leaved plants.
Tip: If at all possible, do not use in aquariums with burrowing or plant-eating fish.

2 *Cabomba caroliniana*
Carolina Fanwort

Family: Cabombaceae.
Range: Northern South America to southern North America.

Appearance: Stem plant; 20 inches (50 cm) tall. Leaves decussate, rarely, triple whorls; leaf blades finely pinnate, leaf segments about 1 millimeter wide, with a median vein. Commercially available in various forms.
Care: Does not tolerate being transplanted, constant trimming, and CO_2 deficiency. Needs clean water and intense light.
Light: 75 watts per 25 gallons (100 L).
Water: 72°–82°F (22°–28°C); 2°–12°dCH; pH 6.5–7.2.
Propagation: By cuttings.
Placement: Use in background, in groups.

Stem Plants

3 The extremely lovely red-violet flower of Cabomba piauhyensis *blooms only briefly. Unfortunately, it is very difficult to get the plant to bloom in an aquarium.*

3 Cabomba piauhyensis *is no plant for beginners.*

3 *Cabomba piauhyensis*

Family: Cambombaceae (watershield family).
Range: Central and South America.
Appearance: Stem plant; about 20 inches (50 cm) tall. Three leaves at each stem node, leaf blades pinnulate, reddish. Floating plants may have floating leaves and very lovely red-violet flowers.
Care: Soft water, strong light (cannot be grown if light is inadequate), and fertilization with iron are absolutely essential! With CO_2 fertilization the water can be somewhat harder. Needs clean water and clean bottom. Keep debris and algae growth under control! Use only gentle fish.

Light: 100 watts per 25 gallons (100 L).
Water: 75°–82°F (24°–28°C); 2°–8°dCH; pH 6.0–6.8.
Propagation: By cuttings.
Placement: Use in groups in the middle or background. Goes well with large-leaved plants.
Tip: *Cabomba piauhyensis* has been used as an aquarium plant only since the 1950s. Like almost all other *Cabomba* species, it is not easy to take care of. Even tiny deviations from its very exacting requirements can result in poor growth. Only with the best lighting conditions, water that is always clean, and a constantly balanced supply of iron will the plant thrive and display a lovely reddish-brown

coloration in the upper stem area. In contrast to many other aquarium plants, *Cabomba piauhyensis*, which prefers soft water, is unable to dissolve out and utilize the carbon dioxide bonded to bicarbonates and carbonates in harder water (see Biogenic decalcification, Glossary). For this reason, carbon dioxide (CO_2) has to be added on a continuous basis if the plant is being grown in fairly hard water. If you can satisfy the high requirements of the *Cabomba* species, you will have an aquarium plant of fascinating beauty in your tank.

Stem Plants

1 Ceratophyllum demersum *is free-floating under the water surface where it forms dense groups.*

2 Didiplis diandra *will flower in the aquarium.*

1 *Ceratophyllum demersum*
Hornwort, Coontail

Family: Ceratophyllaceae (hornwort family).
Range: Worldwide.
Appearance: Stem plant; about 20 inches (50 cm) tall. Rootless plant with dense whorls of forked leaves; leaves dark green, markedly dentate. Free-floating under the water surface, branches to form dense cushions there. Can anchor itself in the bottom with rootlike substitute organs made up of modified leaves. Small flowers in the leaf whorls possible (see photo, inside back cover).
Care: Very thrifty if grown in optimal conditions; thin out regu-

larly to keep it from depriving the bottom-growing plants of light.
Light: 35 watts per 25 gallons (100 L), or more.
Water: 59°–86°F (15°–30°C); (86° for short periods of time); 5°–15°dCH; pH 6.0–7.5.
Propagation: By side shoots.
Placement: Use anywhere in the aquarium.
Tip: Well suited to cold-water tanks and breeding tanks (spawning substrate; hiding places for females that have spawned and for their fry).

2 *Didiplis diandra*
Water Purslane

Family: Lythraceae (loosestrife family).

Range: North America.
Appearance: Stem plant; 6 inches (15 cm) tall. Plants are upright if submersed, creeping if emersed. Leaves decussate, light green; tips of shoots slightly reddish in hue in bright light. Small brownish flowers in the leaf axils, even if grown submersed.
Care: Branches extensively, so don't plant too close together. Good light and regular fertilization (iron) necessary.
Light: 75 watts per 25 gallons (100 L).
Water: 72°–82°F (22°–28°C); 2°–12°dCH; pH 5.8–7.2.
Propagation: By cuttings.
Placement: Use in loose groups in the foreground or middle.

Stem Plants

3 Egeria densa *is a robust plant, good for beginners.*

4 Hemianthus (Micranthemum) micranthemoides.

3 *Egeria densa*
Brazilian Waterweed

Family: Hydrocharitaceae.
Range: Argentina, Paraguay, Brazil.
Appearance: Stem plant; 20 inches (50 cm) tall and more. On free-floating, somewhat brittle stems, light-green whorled leaves, three to five in each whorl. Individual leaves with very finely dentate margins. If daylight strikes floating shoots, whitish flowers will form from time to time.
Care: In a tropical tank, needs regular additions of fertilizer and a great deal of light. With CO_2 fertilization, will thrive even in very hard water.
Light: 50 watts per 25 gallons.

Water: 59°–77°F (15°–25°C); 8°–18°dCH and more; pH 6.5–7.5.
Propagation: By cuttings.
Placement: Use in background and side areas; set in groups.
Tip: Good oxygen producer for all types of aquariums. Also suitable for aquariums with live-bearing toothed carp or American sunfish. Ideal for beginners.

4 *Hemianthus (Micranthemum) micranthemoides*

Family: Scrophulariaceae.
Range: Cuba, southeastern USA.
Appearance: Stem plant; up to 16 inches (40 cm) tall. Grows upright if submersed, creeping if emersed.

Aquatic leaves oblong-oval, sessile, in whorls formed of three or four leaves, light green. Branches well.
Care: Plant in bunches! Needs a great deal of light and regular applications of fertilizer. Sensitive to fish medications and algae control agents that contain try-paflavin.
Light: 75 watts per 25 gallons (100 L), or more.
Water: 72°–82°F (22°–28°C); 2°–12°dCH; pH 6.0–7.0.
Propagation: By cuttings.
Placement: Use in the foreground as a cushion plant (cut back from time to time!) or in the middle as a small hedge. Highly suitable for concealing bare stems of background plants.

Stem Plants

1 Heteranthera zosterifolia *in bloom.*

2 Hydrocotyle leucocephala *is easy to take care of.*

1 *Heteranthera zosterifolia*
Mud Plantain

Family: Pontederiaceae.
Range: Eastern South America.
Appearance: Stem plant; about 20 inches (50 cm) tall. Leaves alternate, sessile, narrow-lanceolate; dense tufts of leaves at the tips of the shoots. Fast-growing, branches develop in large numbers on the floating shoots; blue-violet flowers sometimes form, but only with sun.
Care: After every water change add fertilizer that contains iron!
Light: 75 watts per 25 gallons (100 L).
Water: 72°–82°F (22°–28°C); 3°–15°dCH; pH 6.0–7.5.
Propagation: By cuttings.

Placement: Use along the sides and in the middle and background, growing upright in loose groupings; in the foreground, as a cushion plant.

2 *Hydrocotyle leucocephala* (*Nomaphida corymbosa*)
Water Pennywort

Family: Apiaceae.
Range: Brazil.
Appearance: Stem plant; about 20 inches (50 cm) tall. Leaves alternate, roundish to kidney-shaped with somewhat sinuous margins. Fine roots on the stem nodes.
Care: Grows rapidly; grouping frequently has to be formed anew from tip cuttings; after the cutting

has been taken, the lower portion of the stem that remains rarely produces new shoots, and it is advisable to remove it. Shoots that float at the water surface branch prolifically, thus depriving the other plants of light. For this reason, thin them out regularly! Needs light, otherwise undemanding. White flowers occasionally form in emersed culture and daylight with some sun.
Light: 75 watts per 25 gallons (100 L).
Water: 68°–82°F (20°–28°C); 2°–15°dCH; pH 6.0–7.5.
Propagation: By cuttings.
Placement: Use in groups in the background or along the sides.

Stem Plants

4 Hygrophila difformis, *an undemanding but extremely decorative aquarium plant, is highly recommended for beginners or for newly set-up tanks.*

3 Hygrophila corymbosa has brown stems.

3 Hygrophila corymbosa

Family: Acanthaceae.
Range: India, Malaysia, Indonesia.
Appearance: Stem plant; about 24 inches (60 cm) tall. Leaves decussate, lanceolate, like cherry leaves. Stems brown. Various forms are commercially available.
Care: Grows rapidly, adapts easily, but in overly acidic water the leaves are small, jaundiced, and spotty (like all other *Hygrophila* species). Needs to be fertilized with iron regularly, especially the red-leaved forms, which also require more light than the green ones. Prune regularly and plant cuttings. Branches only after being cut back.

Light: About 50 watts per 25 gallons (100 L).
Water: 72°–82°F (22°–28°C); 2°–15°dCH; pH 6.5–7.5.
Propagation: By cuttings.
Placement: Use in groups in the background and along the sides.

4 Hygrophila difformis
Water Wisteria

Family: Acanthaceae.
Range: India, western Indochina.
Appearance: Stem plant; about 20 inches (50 cm) tall. Leaves decussate, stemmed. Submersed leaves .deeply pinnatisect. Appearance varies. In cold, leaves are small, lobed rather than pinnate; in insufficient light they are only slightly pinnate, and the internodes are long. Roots on the stem nodes. Cultivated form ("green-white") with white leaf venation.
Care: Needs nutrient-rich bottom, regular addition of liquid fertilizer containing iron, and good light; CO_2 fertilization is recommended. Chlorosis develops if iron is in short supply.
Light: 75 watts per 25 gallons (100 L).
Water: 74°–82°F (23°–28°C); 2°–15°dCH; pH 6.5–7.5.
Propagation: By cuttings; by runnerlike side shoots.
Placement: Use in groups in the foreground and middle; in small aquariums also singly.

Stem Plants

2 Limnophila aquatica *will display compact, luxuriant growth only if the light is good and if iron-containing fertilizer is added regularly.*

1 Hygrophila polysperma *branches extensively.*

1 Hygrophila polysperma

Family: Acanthaceae (acanthus family).
Range: India.
Appearance: Stem plant; 24 inches (60 cm) tall. Leaves decussate, lanceolate, green to brownish.
Care: Branches quite extensively, so don't plant too close together. The groups need to be regularly pruned, thinned out, and replaced. Undemanding; regular doses of fertilizer recommended.
Light: 50 watts per 25 gallons (100 L).
Water: 68°–86°F (20°–30°C); 2°–15°dCH; pH 6.5–7.8.
Propagation: By cuttings.

Placement: Use in groups in the center and background.

2 Limnophila aquatica

Family: Scrophulariaceae (figwort family).
Range: India, Sri Lanka.
Appearance: Stem plant; about 20 inches (50 cm) tall. Leaves in whorls of three to twelve, very finely pinnate, the individual leaf segments almost as thin as threads. Well-developed plants up to 5 inches (12 cm) in diameter.
Care: The most demanding of the *Limnophila* species, needs light, grows compact only if light is good. Regular doses of iron neces-

sary! Tolerates soft water better than hard.
Light: 75 watts per 25 gallons (100 L).
Water: 75°–80°F (24°–27°C); 3°–12°dCH; pH 6.5–7.5.
Propagation: By cuttings. Use the upper plant shoot (about 5 inches [12 cm]), because it contains the vegetative cone (see Glossary).
Placement: Recommended only for high aquariums, because in shallow tanks too frequent trimming and new planting results in stunted forms. Looks best in front of a dark background. Goes well with broad-leaved dark-green or red plants.

Stem Plants

3 Don't plant Limnophila sessiliflora *too close together.*

4 Ludwigia repens, *a popular aquarium plant.*

3 *Limnophila sessiliflora*
Ambulia

Family: Scrophulariaceae.
Range: Tropical Southeast Asia.
Appearance: Stem plant; about 20 inches (50 cm) tall. Stem axis with pinnate and furcate leaves, which grow in whorls of 8 to 13. With good light, the stem apexes are slightly reddish.
Care: Regular doses of iron absolutely essential! Great need for light. A location with no shade is important for luxuriant growth. Shoots floating at water surface branch readily, but often become bare lower down. Renovate plantings without delay; don't set groups too close together!
Light: 75 watts per 25 gallons (100 L).
Water: 72°–82°F (22°–28°C); 3°–15°dCH; pH 6.0–7.5.
Propagation: By cuttings.
Placement: Use in groups in the middle and foreground.

4 *Ludwigia repens*
Water Primrose

Family: Onagraceae.
Range: Tropical North America and Central America.
Appearance: Stem plant; about 20 inches (50 cm) tall. Leaves decussate, short-stemmed, roundish to broad-ovate; upper side olive-green, underside reddish to deep red. Color is dependent on light; in weak light the plants remain pale. In emersed culture, small flowers with yellow petals may form.
Care: Tolerates coolish water better than overly warm; needs nutrient-rich bottom and regular additions of fertilizer after every water change. Branches prolifically, so be sure to leave enough room at the sides when planting!
Light: 50 watts per 25 gallons (100 L).
Water: 68°–86°F (20°–30°C); 2°–15°dCH; pH 5.5–7.5.
Propagation: By cuttings.
Placement: Use in groups in the middle and along the sides.

Stem Plants

2 Rotala macrandra *will turn green if the light is weak. With good light and regular doses of iron, the red color will be retained.*

1 Myriophyllum aquaticum *is a good spawning plant for fish.*

1 *Myriophyllum aquaticum*
Water Milfoil, Parrot's Feather

Family: Haloragaceae .
Range: South America, naturalized in southern North America.
Appearance: Stem plant; 20 inches (50 cm) tall. Stem axis branches. Pinnulate aquatic leaves in whorls of three to six. Shoot tips reddish if light is good. Shoots that float at the water surface may form comb-like, coarse aerial leaves.
Similar species: Myriophyllum matogrossense—smaller; with intense light levels and use of iron-containing fertilizer, leaflets are red-brown.
Care: Do not prune these plants too often, but do thin out before they take too much light away from the plants growing at the bottom! Fertilization and addition of CO_2 will promote vigorous growth.
Light: About 50 watts per 25 gallons (100 L).
Water: 64°–86°F (18°–30°C); 2°–15°dCH; pH 5.0–7.5.
Propagation: By cuttings.
Placement: Groups in background.
Tip: Good spawning plant for fish.

2 *Rotala macrandra*
Tooth-cup

Family: Lythraceae.
Range: India.
Appearance: Stem plant; 20 inches (50 cm) tall. Leaves decussate, sessile, broad-ovate to elliptical, olive-brown to dark red-brown.
Care: Stems and leaves sensitive to pressure. Susceptible to being eaten by snails. Strong light, fertilized bottom, and regular doses of iron are essential to maintain and intensify the red color. Plants turn green in weak light. Moving water and low pH are also good for the red color.
Light: 75 watts per 25 gallons (100 L).
Water: 77°–86°F (25°–30°C); 2°–15°dCH; pH 6.0–7.0.
Propagation: By cuttings.
Placement: Use in groups as a focal point.
Tip: Don't use in aquariums with lively, burrowing fish.

Stem Plants

3 Rotala rotundifolia *is an adaptable plant.*

4 Shinnersia rivularis *grows over 40 inches (100 cm) tall.*

3 *Rotala rotundifolia*
Tooth-cup

Family: Lythraceae.
Range: Mainland of Southeast Asia.
Appearance: Stem plant; about 20 inches (50 cm) tall. If submersed, growth is upright; if emersed, creeping. Leaves decussate, shape variable, usually oblong-oval, also narrow-lanceolate or almost round. *Similar species: Rotala wallichii—* leaflets needle-shaped, fine as hairs, whorled. Care similar to that required for *Rotala rotundifolia,* but it needs soft water and pH of 5.0–6.5.
Care: Bottom fertilization, regular water changes, and liquid fertilizer containing iron are necessary for brisk growth and reddish color.
Light: 50 watts per 25 gallons (100 L).
Water: 68°–86°F (20°–30°C); 2°–15°dCH; pH 5.5–7.2.
Propagation: By cuttings.
Placement: Use in groups in middle and background.

4 *Shinnersia rivularis*

Family: Asteraceae.
Range: Northern Mexico.
Appearance: Stem plant; 40 inches (100 cm) tall and more. Leaves decussate, along the margins repeatedly sinuous or rather deeply lobed, rich green. Grows very rapidly (up to 16 inches [40 cm] per week), forms long internodes; only near the light source do the leaves become denser. The shoots float and branch; new shoots branch throughout the entire length of the stem axis.
Care: Undemanding. Recommended only for large aquariums; otherwise, weekly thinning out is absolutely essential (but soon results in stunted growth).
Light: 75 watts per 25 gallons (100 L).
Water: 68°–82°F (20°–28°C); 2°–15°dCH; pH 5.5–7.5.
Propagation: By cuttings.
Placement: Use in thickets.

Ferns

1 *Tie* Bolbitis heudelotii *to roots or rocks.*

2 Ceratopteris thalictroides *reproduces well.*

1 *Bolbitis heudelotii*

Family: Aspleniaceae or Lomariopsidaceae (finger fern family).
Range: Ethiopia to South Africa.
Appearance: Fern; in the wild up to 20 inches (50 cm) tall; in the aquarium often only 8 inches (20 cm) tall. Creeping rhizome. Leaves stemmed, dark green, hard, somewhat brittle; leaf blade lobed and pinnate. Grows outdoors in the spray zone of rushing streams. Rooted underwater, leaves emersed, completely submerged during the rainy season.
Care: Tie rhizome to root wood or stone (lava). For submersed culture, the plant requires clean, moving water and from time to time some fertilizer.
Light: 30 watts per 25 gallons (100 L).
Water: 72°–79°F (22°–26°C); 2°–12°dCH; pH 5.8–7.0.
Propagation: By rhizome division or by side sprouts on the rhizome.
Placement: Use singly or in shaded places in the background or along the sides.

2 *Ceratopteris thalictroides* Oriental Water Fern

Family: Parkeriaceae (water fern family).
Range: Tropics, worldwide.
Appearance: Fern; up to 20 inches (50 cm) tall. Dense rosette, light green, leaf blades deeply pinnatisect. Large, finely branched roots. *Ceratopteris cornuta* and *Ceratopteris pteridoides* often are called merely growth forms of *Ceratopteris thalictroides*.
Care: Grows rapidly in well-fertilized water, reproduces readily. Don't plant too deep; the point where the roots begin has to be visible above the bottom material.
Light: 50 watts per 25 gallons (100 L).
Water: 72°–86°F (22°–30°C); 5°–15°dCH; pH 6.5–7.5.
Propagation: By adventitious plants on the leaf margins; quite productive.
Placement: Use singly; in large aquariums place in groups in the background.

Fern/Liverwort/Moss

4 Riccia fluitans.

3 Microsorium pteropus *is well suited for aquariums where cichlids live.*

5 Vesicularia dubyana.

3 *Microsorium pteropus*
Java Fern

Family: Polypodiaceae.
Range: Tropical Southeast Asia.
Appearance: Fern; about 8 inches (20 cm) tall. Rhizome creeping, green. Leaves single, stemmed, lanceolate, rarely trilobate.
Care: Don't plant rhizome, tie it to wood or rocks.
Light: 30 watts per 25 gallons (100 L).
Water: 68°–82°F (20°–28°C); 2°–12°dCH; pH 5.5–7.5.
Propagation: By adventitious plants on leaves and roots; rhizome division also possible.
Placement: Singly or in groups.

4 *Riccia fluitans*
Crystalwort

Family: Ricciaceae.
Range: Worldwide.
Appearance: Moss; length of thallus (vegetative body) about 0.8 inch (2 cm). Floating plant or clinging to a substrate. Thallus is flat, forked, often matted with others to form dense cushions.
Care: Undemanding; thin out regularly. Will not tolerate extremely soft, nutrient-poor water. Avoid vigorous agitation of water.
Light: 50 watts per 25 gallons (100 L), or less.
Water: 59°–86°F (15°–30°C); 5°–15°dCH; pH 6.0–8.0.
Propagation: By cushion division.

5 *Vesicularia dubyana*
Java Moss

Family: Hypnaceae.
Range: India, Malaya, Java.
Appearance: Moss with thin stem and two rows of tiny lanceolate leaves. Individual leaflets up to 4 millimeters long. Uses its rhizoids to cling. Branches prolifically and forms dense cushions.
Care: Planting not necessary; undemanding.
Light: About 25 watts per 25 gallons (100 L).
Water: 68°–86°F (20°–30°C); 2°–15°dCH; pH 5.8–7.5.
Propagation: By cushion division.
Tip: Makes a good spawning plant for bottom-spawning fish.

Index

The numbers in **bold** type refer to photographs.

Photos on the Covers

Front cover: Amazon swordplant.
Inside front cover: Dutch aquarium.
Inside back cover: Aquarium plants and their flowers.
Back cover: Aquarium with luxuriant plantings.

Important Notes

Electrical appliances for use in aquarium maintenance are described in this book. Always follow the instructions shown on page 19 (*Safety in the Aquarium Area*). Otherwise, extremely serious accidents may occur.
Before buying a large aquarium, test the load-bearing capacity of the floor at the place where you intend to put the tank.
Water damage caused by broken glass, overflow, or leaks that develop in the tank cannot always be avoided. For this reason, be sure to obtain insurance coverage (see page 19).
Make absolutely sure that children (and adults) do not eat any of the aquarium plants. Otherwise, their health could be seriously impaired.

The Author

Ines Scheurmann, born in 1950, has a degree in Biology (field of specialty: The Behavior of Fish). She has many years of experience in keeping and breeding aquarium plants and fish. She is the author of the aquarium guides *An Aquarium for Freshwater Fish and Plants* and *Breeding Aquarium Fish*.

The Photographers

Nieuwenhuizen: Inside front cover

and pages 1, 4, 12, 24, 25, 40, 41, 64, 72 left, 80 right, 83 right, 84 right, 86 right, 89 above right, back cover. Reinhard: Page 17. Kahl: All other photos.

Useful Books

For further reading on this subject and related matter, consult the following books also published by Barron's Educational Series, Inc., Hauppauge, New York:
Blasiola, G: *The New Saltwater Aquarium Handbook*, 1991.
Giovanette, TA: *Discus Fish*, 1991.
Hellner, S: *Killifish*, 1990.
Ostrow, ME: *Goldfish*, 1985.
Penzes, B, Tolg, I: *Goldfish and Ornamental Carp*, 1986.
Scheurmann, I: *Aquarium Fish Breeding*, 1990.
Scheurmann, I: *The New Aquarium Fish Handbook*, 1986.
Scheurmann, I: *Water Plants in the Aquarium*, 1987.
Schliewen, U: *Aquarium Fish*, 1992.
Stadelmann, P: *Tropical Fish*, 1991.
Ward, B: *The Aquarium Fish Survival Manual*, 1985.

© Copyright 1992 by Gräfe und Unzer GmbH, Munich.
The title of the German book is *Pflanzen fürs Aquarium*.
Translated from the German by Kathleen Luft.

First English language edition published in 1993 by Barron's Educational Series, Inc. English translation © Copyright 1993 by Barron's Educational Series, Inc.

Address all inquiries to:
Barron's Educational Series, Inc.
250 Wireless Boulevard
Hauppauge, New York 11788.

Library of Congress Catalog Card No. 93-10733
International Standard Book No. 0-8120-1687-4
Printed in Hong Kong.

Library of Congress Cataloging-in-Publication Data

Scheurmann, Ines, 1950–
[Pflanzen fürs Aquarium. English]
Aquarium plants manual : selecting and maintaining water plants in large and small aquariums / Ines Scheurmann ; with color photographs by Burkard Kahl and A. van den Nieuwenhuizen ; and drawings by Marlene Gemke ; consulting editor, Dennis W. Stevenson ; [translated from the German by Kathleen Luft].
p.   cm.
Includes bibliographical references (p.   ) and index.
ISBN 0-8120-1687-4
1. Aquarium plants--Handbooks, manuals, etc.   I. Stevenson, Dennis W.
II. Title.
SF457.7.S32513 1993   93-10733
635.9'674--dc20   CIP

BARRON'S PREMIUM PET CARE SERIES

* One-volume, all inclusive hardcover & paperback reference books
* Illustrated with from 35 to 200 stunning full-color photos, plus numerous drawings and charts.

AQUARIUM FISH SURVIVAL MANUAL, THE
by Ward. A directory of more than 300 marine and freshwater fish species, including a guide to aquatic plants. 176 pp., 7¾" × 10", (0-8120-9391-7) Paperback.

AQUARIUM FISH BREEDING by Scheurmann. Dozens of fish species are described, and their mating habits outlined. 30 beautiful full-color photos and dozens of finely-detailed line drawings. 144 pp., 6½" × 7⅞", (0-8120-4474-6) Paperback.

BEST PET NAME BOOK EVER, THE by Eldridge. Presents 22 lists of names —1500 in all to help give a pet the best name ever. 208 pp., 6¹⁵/₁₆" × 6¹⁵/₁₆", (0-8120-9661-4) Paperback.

THE COMPLETE BOOK OF BUDGERIGARS
by B. Moizer & S. Moizer. The definitive reference on one of the world's most popular pets—Budgerigars (e.g. Parakeets). 144 pp., 8" × 11¼", (0-8120-6059-8) Hardcover.

CARING FOR YOUR OLDER DOG by Pinney. Advice on diet, exercise, general health measures for older dogs—and information about diseases to which they are prone. 192 pp., 6½" × 7⅞", (0-8120-9149-3) Paperback.

THE CAT CARE MANUAL by Viner. Shows you how to meet all the needs of your cat and helps you understand its behavior. 160 pp., 7⅝" × 9¹³/₁₆", (0-8120-1767-6) Paperback.

COMMUNICATING WITH YOUR DOG by Baer. How to train your dog intelligently and humanely. 144 pp., 6½" × 7⅞", (0-8120-4203-4) Paperback.

COMPLETE BOOK OF CAT CARE, THE
by Behrend & Wegler. Many vivid full-color photos of different cats, plus expert advice on selecting, breeding, feeding, health care, and more. 144 pp., 6⅝" × 9¼", (0-8120-4613-7) Paperback.

COMPLETE BOOK OF DOG CARE, THE
by Klever. Dog-care expert answers questions about selecting, training, grooming and health care. 176 pp., 6⅝" × 9¼", (0-8120-4158-5) Paperback.

THE DOG CARE MANUAL by Alderton. Gives you expert pointers on the general and medical care of your dog, as well as on obedience training. 160 pp., 7⅝" × 9¹³/₁₆", (0-8120-9163-9) Paperback.

GOLDFISH AND ORNAMENTAL CARP
by Penzes & Tölg. Covers everything from anatomy, biology and varieties to nutrition, "housing" and diseases. 136 pp., 7¾" × 10", (0-8120-9286-4) Paperback.

HEALTHY CAT, HAPPY CAT by Müller and Müller. Explanations of general health and safety measures, advice on protecting against parasites, accident prevention and first-aid treatment. 128 pp., 6½" × 7⅞", (0-8120-9136-1) Paperback.

THE HORSE CARE MANUAL by May. A veterinary surgeon covers all facets of horse and pony ownership, through a convenient question-and-answer format. 160 pp., 7½" × 9¾", (0-8120-1133-3) Paperback.

LABYRINTH FISH by Pinter. Teaches you about the feeding, breeding, and diseases of these fish and about aquarium maintenance. 136 pp., 7¾" × 10", (0-8120-5635-3) Hardcover.

NONVENOMOUS SNAKES by Trutnau. Features detailed descriptions of over 100 snake species and covers feeding, breeding, illnesses, and terrariums. 192 pp., 7¾" × 10", (0-8120-5632-9) Hardcover.

Barron's Educational Series, Inc. • 250 Wireless Boulevard • Hauppauge, New York 11788
• For sales information call toll-free: 1-800-645-3476.
In Canada: Georgetown Book Warehouse • 34 Armstrong Avenue
Georgetown, Ontario L7G 4R9 • Call toll-free: 1-800-247-7160

Order these titles from your favorite bookstore or pet shop.

(#65) R 2/97

Ammannia gracilis, *flower.*

Ammannia gracilis.

Aponogeton madagascariensis.

Aponogeton mad., *flower.*

Getting plants to bloom in an aquarium is a delightful notion, but not that easy to bring about. Many plants will flower only above water, and most have to be pollinated "by hand" (see page 44). In any event, growing the plants in optimal conditions is the most vital prerequisite for success.

Cabomba aquatica, *flower.*

Cabomba caroliniana, *flower.*